**Travel Instruction** _____

**for the Handicapped** _____

... The fact that Peter learned to use the public transit is really a miraculous thing for our family because our expectations were not high. It was a thrill to find that they have been stretched. To find that reality has stretched and reached beyond what expectations are. Peter's done a thing that I never dreamed he would do. It changed my perception of him ...

... The orientation and mobility program resulted in a whole new lease on life for Peter. It is as major as toilet training or feeding for retarded people. Toilet training and self-feeding are those beginning steps in independence, and this is really the step into adulthood ...

Exerpts from a Parent Interview

# Travel Instruction ▬▬▬
# for the Handicapped ▬▬

*By*

**MICHAEL D. LAUS, B.S., M.Ed.**

*Orientation and Mobility Specialist*
*Pittsburgh Public Schools*
*Pittsburgh, Pennsylvania*

*With a Foreword by*

**Barry Head**

*Family Communications, Inc.*
*Pittsburgh, Pennsylvania*

**CHARLES C THOMAS • PUBLISHER**
*Springfield • Illinois • U.S.A.*

*Published and Distributed Throughout the World by*
CHARLES C THOMAS ● PUBLISHER
Bannerstone House
301-327 East Lawrence Avenue, Springfield, Illinois, U.S.A.

© *1977, by* CHARLES C THOMAS ● PUBLISHER

ISBN 0-398-03637-3

Library of Congress Catalog Card Number: 76-39948

*With* THOMAS BOOKS *careful attention is given to all details of manufacturing and design. It is the Publisher's desire to present books that are satisfactory as to their physical qualities and artistic possibilities and appropriate for their particular use.* THOMAS BOOKS *will be true to those laws of quality that assure a good name and good will.*

*Printed in the United States of America*
*R-1*

*Library of Congress Cataloging in Publication Data*

Laus, Michael D
  Travel instruction for the handicapped.

  Bibliography: p.
  1. Mentally handicapped--Transportation--United
States.  I. Title.
HV3005.5.L38        371.9′24        76-39948
ISBN 0-398-03637-3

*To my wife, Jan,*
*children Kristin and Michael,*
*and my mother and father for their*
*love, support, and encouragement.*

# FOREWORD

IF you like watching people, Sixth and Wood in downtown Pittsburgh is a good place to stand in the early morning. As the business day begins, tycoons, secretaries, young executives, delivery boys, matrons and merchants, the overfed and the underprivileged converge here, mingle, and disperse again on their way to work.

They come from all quarters of the city and the suburbs beyond. For some, downtown is the final destination. For others, it is just a transfer stop to a more distant end point. The general bustle of alighting and boarding, of crossing and dodging is typical of most major cities. Rush hour in Pittsburgh is brusque and purposeful. Pittsburgh is, after all, a city where decisions profoundly affecting the national economy are made as routinely as the chiming of the Trinity Cathedral clock. You can't dawdle here and expect the rest of the city to wait for you to catch up.

Among the transients moving through downtown during the morning rush are many citizens that have been labeled as trainable mentally retarded. Most are headed for a special school, within the Pittsburgh Public School System, located on the north side of the city. Each morning, they do what is routine for most people but unthinkable for handicapped persons in most communities: They walk from home to their bus stops, board the correct bus, disembark downtown at the right stop, walk two or three zig-zag blocks ... and about 8:15 AM any weekday you can see them gather under the Joseph Horne marquee waiting for a 16E to come by and take them the rest of the way to school. If you watch carefully, you may be able to spot others in the crowd; several of the school's graduates are now following new bus routes to places of salaried employment.

This unobtrusive integration of the handicapped into the mainstream of society is one of those quiet phenomena with profound consequences. Participating in this program has opened to the retarded themselves a whole new range of activities made possible by increased mobility. They have acquired a number of new skills in the process of learning to travel independently that can serve them in performing other daily tasks. Their success in learning these skills and the resulting rewards of independence have markedly affected their pride, confidence, and motivation.

The effects on the parents of the travelers have been no less significant. Many, for the first time in years, have begun again to regard their handicapped children as capable of learning. Some who had long since become resigned to the total dependence of their children have renewed their commitment to helping their children cope for themselves. These parents have found pride in their children's accomplishments and, inevitably, new hope that other long-accepted limitations on their lives and on the lives of their children may not have to be accepted after all.

And for the Pittsburgh Public School System, the payoff of the program has been dramatic in another way. After the mobility training program had been implemented for only one year, thirty-five students were coming and going by public bus transportation instead of leased conveyances. This resulted in a savings of $20,000 in transportation fees.

This program has been run almost entirely by one man, Michael D. Laus. It has been functioning now for four years. More than 100 trainable mentally retarded young people, many with other secondary handicaps, are now using public transportation for a variety of purposes — confidently and without incident. It seems time to let others know what can be done, to encourage others to do it, and to provide these others with the knowledge and tools to help them do it successfully. This book is the first step in this direction.

Barry Head
Family Communications, Inc.

# PREFACE

     A BASIC skill required for citizens within our society is the ability to travel independently within the community. In order to fulfill basic needs and to strive toward self-actualization, citizens in this complex society move about and interact with their environment. People travel daily to go to work, to shop, to socialize, and to engage in leisure-time activities.

    The person with no serious impairments has the ability to travel independently within his environment; this ability develops naturally as the individual grows. The young child learns to crawl, to walk, to negotiate stairs safely, and to move freely within his home. Gradually the child learns to cross residential streets independently and becomes mobile in his neighborhood. By adolescence, the young person is able to use public transportation and eventually is permitted to drive an automobile. This complex developmental process normally unfolds without formal, planned, learning experiences.

    However, when a person is impaired by a sensory loss, physical disability, subnormal cognitive functioning, low societal expectations, or a combination of these problems, he may not be able to travel independently without assistance from a structured, developmental learning program.

    Formal travel instruction for the blind has been the first of these training programs to develop. It teaches blind persons to travel independently within the community. This structured, developmental learning program teaches blind persons, with assistance from either a cane or guide dog, to travel safely and independently indoors, in residential areas, and business areas. The developmental process teaches skills in negotiating sidewalks, stairs, stop sign-controlled intersections, traffic light-controlled intersections, and public transit facilities. As a result of this formalized instructional process, blind persons learn to travel safely, independently, and comfortably within the community.

The impetus to develop formalized programs for serving the needs of blind persons in the United States was provided by blind veterans of two world wars. Standardized mobility devices and procedures for teaching travel skills to blind veterans resulted from both wars. Formalized training of dogs as mobility aids developed in Germany during World War I; the use of the Hoover Cane Technique, the basis for cane use today, was developed to serve blind veterans from World War II (Ball, 1964).

In 1960 and 1961, Boston College and Western University, respectively, began the first professional programs to train instructors to teach independent travel skills to the blind. Since that time, other similar university programs have developed across the United States. Although it was not until the 1960s that university programs were established to professionally train orientation and mobility instructors for the blind, these programs have succeeded in raising the professional standards of travel instruction. In addition, these university programs have served as centers involved in research as well as program development.

Nevertheless, little has been done to deal with the travel needs of impaired persons other than the blind. A 1972 publication of the President's Committee on Mental Retardation, *Transportation and the Mentally Retarded,* concluded that programs teaching independent travel skills in the use of public transportation facilities to mentally retarded persons were generally lacking. The study reported that:

> the majority of agencies [serving mentally retarded persons]
> do not expect individuals to be capable of independent travel
> and consequently, they are not capable [p. 17].

This study identified problems in the establishment of programs to teach mentally retarded persons to travel: (1) little awareness that it can be done, (2) inadequate public transportation facilities, and (3) insufficient numbers of instructors to teach mentally retarded persons. The President's Committee on

Mental Retardation (1972) has recommended that we must modify our perceptions of the capability of mentally retarded persons for independent travel.

This book is a beginning step designed to fulfill this need. It is a model that provides a rationale and guide for the implementation of a structured learning program to teach sighted but cognitively impaired persons to travel safely, independently, and comfortably within the community. This work is based on my design and implementation of an established program in a public school setting where sighted but cognitively impaired pupils have learned to utilize public transportation facilities in order to travel independently. These pupils have been labeled as trainable mentally retarded as the result of their intelligence test performances. Furthermore, concomitant with this label, many of this population are impaired by brain injury, physical handicap, deafness, speech impairment, emotional disturbance, and, above all, by low societal expectations. While the focus of this book deals with a program designed for pupils whose primary disability label is that of trainable mentally retarded, I perceive this work as a model whereby professionals as well as parents can modify its contents to be of significant use for persons regardless of the impairment or complexity of impairments.

The message of this book is that when many of these cognitively impaired persons are provided with an appropriate training program, they are able to learn independent travel; many have already learned independent travel skills, and now we ought to expect many more to travel independently. This book concludes that independent travel instruction must be considered an integral part of services for cognitively impaired persons in the following settings: public schools, sheltered workshops, activity centers, group homes, rehabilitation centers, and state institutions. It is written for teachers, supervisors, and administrators in these settings as well as college students, parent organizations, and parents — people who are concerned with the reduction of dependence and the normalization of cognitively impaired persons. It is based on the assumption that if we raise our expectations, we will raise performance. For too long, we have expected little of cognitively impaired persons, and their development has met our expectations.

Chapter 1 critically reviews those programs that have reported success in teaching mentally retarded persons to travel independently. This analysis provides the reader with background data that may be of value in future program development, and it gives credit to the early pioneers of travel instruction for the mentally retarded.

Chapter 2 begins a descriptive analysis of my travel instruction program in the Pittsburgh Public School System. It describes the setting that provides a context for the establishment of the travel instruction program; it discusses the consideration of the risk involved in such a program; and it defines the basic goal, which is to teach pupils one basic public transit route to enable them to travel to school daily in lieu of taxicabs and leased vans. In addition, it discusses aspects of my program that were adapted from other ones which teach travel to the blind.

Chapters 3 and 4 discuss the process involved in identifying candidates for travel instruction and in gaining parental support and commitment. Both chapters include case studies that further explicate the process through real situations.

Chapter 5 provides a theoretical framework for the actual instruction of pupils, and Chapter 6 is a case study that follows a pupil through the instructional process elucidated in the previous chapter. These two chapters present the theory and then provide examples from real situations that describe the practice of this theory.

Chapter 7 reports the results of the Pittsburgh program and discusses prescriptions for future programming efforts.

Chapter 8 presents a series of anecdotes that give the reader insight into the problems, hassles, and joys of a travel instruction program.

Finally, the parents of the pupils involved in travel instruction are given the opportunity to speak in Chapter 9. The chapter is comprised of verbatim interviews with parents who candidly discuss, in retrospect, their fears and joys.

M.D.L.

# ACKNOWLEDGMENTS ─────────────────

LIFE offers many paths to choose and to follow. My life's direction has been guided by the fortuitous meeting of many diverse people. I think my mother was right when she said many times throughout the years that "You are a reflection of your friends." I would like to take this opportunity to thank the following who have helped me find my way: Doctor Robert Dickie, Jack the Mountain Weatherman, Earl the Candlemaker, Uncle Tony, Regis-Rent-A-Party, the Penn Hills Pepperonis Bocce Club, Willie Johnston, Don Wonderling, Jim Morgan, Rich Cechetti, Uncle Chub, Doctor L. Leon Reid, Johnny Creed Crow, Paul Lewis, Doctor Ruth L. Scott, Tippy Dye, Tooty's Pizza Shop, Tinkerbell, The Big O, Tom Fernekes, Leo Buscaglia, Ron Conant, Elsie Neal, Harold Neal, Barry Head, and Edward Gaw.

I would like to thank Earl Cohen, Laurie Cohen, and Judith Stanfield who worked many hours editing my manuscript.

A special thanks goes to my trusted friend David Champagne, for without his friendship, guidance, and concern this book would still be a fantasy.

M.D.L.

# CONTENTS

# Travel Instruction
## for the Handicapped

# Chapter 1

# A CRITICAL REVIEW
# OF EARLY PROGRAMS

> When we take a man as he is, we make him worse; but when
> we take a man as if he were already what he should be, we
> promote him to what he can be.
>
> Goethe

COGNITIVELY impaired persons tradition-
ally have not been expected to be capable of independent travel.
Although professionals take pride in teaching these persons
basic academic skills, self-help skills, socialization skills, motor
skills, and vocational skills in order to function in a supervised
work setting, they still permit these pupils and workers to be
transported daily to school or work by privately leased conveyances or by parents. Programs have been preparing pupils or
clients to be workers, but they are not teaching basic skills that
permit them to travel independently to work.

As it has taken many years for the establishment of professional programs to teach blind persons to travel, professionals
concerned with sighted handicapped persons have only recently
begun to be aware of a similar need for a specialized program
to teach travel skills. A few professionals have reported formal
learning programs that have been developed to teach independent travel skills to the mentally retarded: Tobias (1963),
Cortazzo and Sansone (1969), Kubat (1973), and Laus (1974). In
this first chapter, I make a critical examination of the first three
of these programs. This critical review can provide the basis for
future program development.

## THE TOBIAS PROGRAM

In 1963, J. Tobias reported that the Sheltered Workshop of

the Association for Helping Retarded Children in New York City provided travel training for its trainable mentally retarded clients to enable them to travel independently to work. It was made explicit from the very first contact with prospective clients that they were expected to learn to travel alone to the workshop. While the agency assisted in training, no transportation was provided for clients, and it was the parents' responsibility to arrange daily attendance to the sheltered workshop. Tobias (1963) reported that the workshop population was generally successful in meeting these expectations.

However, Tobias found that the Occupational Day Center, another division of the Association for Helping Retarded Children in New York City, did not, upon admission, set similar expectations for the independent travel of its clients. Bus service to pick up and return clients daily was chartered by the agency from the inception of the program. The chartered service seemed necessary in that only nine admissions of the total of eighty-three were able to travel independently (Tobias, 1963).

Although there was disagreement among the staff, it was decided that the clients of the Occupational Day Center should receive travel training so that they, like the analogous group of Sheltered Workshop clients, could travel independently to the Center via public transit. Some staff members were concerned about the feasibility of developing the skill of independent travel. Tobias (1963) asked:

> Is the specific lack of ability an inevitable consequence of retardation or is it a result of defects in education? External restrictions that had been imposed on some trainees as necessary conditions of adaptations to a family situation result in ingrained patterns of behavior that are interpreted as natural results of the intellectual deficit. It becomes difficult to distinguish between the incapacity that results from inadequate training, from specific prohibitions, or from mental deficiency. Training programs should attempt to make these distinctions [p. 36].

When the parents of the Center's clients were contacted, they overwhelmingly rejected travel training as unfeasible despite discussions of the self-evident advantages of independent travel

(Tobias, 1963). Many parents considered the whole idea inappropriate, and some even suggested that the staff was naive to consider that their offspring would have the ability to perform such a task.

Tobias (1963) reported that a series of group sessions were arranged to discuss the advantages of travel training and to allay parental fears. The sessions resulted in no general approval by parents for establishing a travel training program. The outcomes of the sessions were the antithesis of what Tobias had intended; the sessions tended to reinforce the parents' objections (1963).

To offset this impasse of parental objection, Tobias used a different strategy. He selected a high-functioning client who possessed the prerequisite academic skills, social maturity, and emotional readiness for success to receive travel training. This client's parents readily accepted the judgment of the staff and gave permission for their son to receive travel instruction.

For this initial client, Tobias (1963) developed the following procedures that subsequently have been applied to all other travel training candidates:

1. An individual member of staff was assigned as a personal tutor to accompany the trainee from and to his home by the most suitable public transportation.
2. The staff member assumed responsibility for the safety of the trainee.
3. Assurances were given to the parents that self-travel would not be permitted until mastery of the route was perfected [p. 38].

These three points appear to be critical to the success of a travel training program. A one-to-one teaching relationship is vital, for each client must learn a unique daily travel route. In addition, such a ratio insures a safe instructional process. Having one instructor throughout the learning experience is vital if there is to be continuity of instruction. Since the client will be supervised by one instructor, an informed judgment can be made of a client's mastery of the travel route.

The success of this initial client resulted in other parents reappraising their own attitudes toward permitting their child to participate in travel training. After this initial breakthrough, fifty out of a total eighty-three clients achieved independence in their travel to and from the Occupational Day Center and their home. As a result of an appropriate training program, the mentally retarded clients demonstrated that the lack of travel skills was a result of defects in their education. From this experience, Tobias (1963) suggested the following practices be generalized for all clients receiving travel instruction:

1. Reducing parental anxiety by constant reassurance of personal safety through close supervision by a staff member.
2. Reinforcement of reluctant approval through sharing with the parents each instance of successful achievement.
3. Reducing trainee's anxiety by verbal reassurance and direct assistance as long as it seems necessary. Rewarding partial success by praise and the final achievement by a 'diploma' presented in public to the applause of peers.
4. The training process must be attuned to the slow acquisition of cues that have relevance for the trainee. Appropriate landmarks, i.e. 'colored lights,' 'furniture store,' 'A&P,' 'hot dog stand,' must be substituted for printed signs. The most limited literacy must be utilized even when it involves only initial letters or numerical designations.
5. Special difficulties such as pushing through turnstiles, inattentiveness, lack of ability to identify coins, etc., must be overcome through special tutoring [p. 178].

These generalized practices seem necessary and important parts of their training program and of any training program.

Tobias (1963) found that there was a highly significant relationship between intelligence test scores and the ability to benefit from travel training. Of the fifty clients out of eighty-three who learned to travel independently, the IQ range was 20 to 65, with a mean of 43.8. The twenty-four trainees who were not able to benefit from travel instruction had IQ scores ranging from 17 to 44, with a mean of 27.6. Tobias listed the following factors that prevented success in the twenty-four clients in the nontraveler group:

1. The profoundly retarded, generally with IQs below 30, who have limited speech and striking incompetences in most other functions. n = 4.
2. Severe seizure cases. n = 2.
3. Adamant parental refusal to permit self-travel. A number of trainees who have mastered travel skills are denied permission by parents to use public facilities. n = 6.
4. Withdrawal from self-travel after successful training because of socially unacceptable incidents in the subway. n = 2 [p. 181].

Despite the obvious statistical difference between the two groups, there was no indication of the amount of effort or types of experiences provided in attempt to train those in the nontraveler group. The element of staff self-fulfilling prophecy might be considered. Did those in the nontraveler group fail because of their low IQs, or did staff members presuppose that those with low IQs would fail?

While Tobias did not discuss this factor, he did summarize his report by saying that although there is a significant relationship between intelligence and travel ability, the level of intelligence required has been generally overestimated (1963). Travel instruction, he continued, was proven feasible with many under the IQ level of 35.

## THE CORTAZZO AND SANSONE PROGRAM

In a program which was similar to Tobias' but structured on a broader scale, A. C. Cortazzo and R. Sansone (1969) described the success of eight activity centers, located in different parts of the United States, in teaching independent travel skills to trainable mentally retarded adult clients. Of the 378 clients, whose ages ranged from seventeen to forty, with a mean chronological age of twenty-one, 199 learned to travel independently. The IQ range was 12 to 55, with the mean of 33. Cortazzo and Sansone (1969) listed seven major phases of their travel training program:

1. Selection of trainees
2. Teaching identification fact-skills
3. Teaching pedestrian techniques
4. Teaching the travel route
5. Teaching the handling of money
6. Teaching conveyance identification
7. Parent counseling [p. 69].

Although the authors listed these seven phases separately, they stated that most of them are carried out simultaneously. Each of the seven phases are reviewed critically in the following section.

## Selection of Trainees

Due to the critical nature of the activity and dangers implicit in such a program, Cortazzo and Sansone (1969) believed that selection of clients for travel instruction was a vital concern. They believed that early success with the first few clients would be crucial to success of the total travel training program. Candidate selection was based on a high rating of the clients on the following criteria (1969):

1. Level of intellectual functioning as indicated on previously administered psychological tests
   a. An IQ of 30 or above on the WAIS or the Stanford-Binet, the Goodenough Draw-a-Man Test, and the Peabody Picture Vocabulary Test.
   b. A Social Quotient of 30 or above on the Vineland Social Maturity Scale
   c. A relatively stable picture on the Functional Check List of Personal and Social Skills developed at the Center
2. Good physical appearance and freedom from the following gross secondary handicaps
   a. Physical stigmata
   b. Epilepsy
   c. Orthopedic defects
   d. Visual defects
   e. Auditory defects

    f. Heart defects
3. Social maturity
    a. Assumes responsibility in the program and at home
    b. Is dependable in carrying out assignments
    c. Follows a set of instructions
    d. Acts independently without being prompted
    e. Gets along well with trainees and staff
    f. Seeks aid from policemen or other community helpers
4. Emotional stability
    a. Does not panic easily
    b. Is free from phobias (Many severely retarded trainees had irrational fears, e.g. dogs, cats, pigeons, dark, etc.)
    c. Is free from offensive habits, e.g. autistic like behavior, teeth grinding, genital play, effusiveness, etc.
    d. Does not seek attention nor is easily led
    e. Takes failures, and frustration tolerance threshold is fairly high
5. Communication skills
    a. Uses intelligible speech-sentences preferred
    b. Uses ID card
    c. Uses telephone
    d. Comprehends directions
    e. Remembers directions
    f. Takes appropriate communicative actions
6. Degree of independence
    a. Takes care of his own personal needs
    b. Takes care of his own room and other household chores
    c. Moves freely about immediate vicinity of home and neighborhood
    d. Goes on simple errands for parents and neighbors
    e. Can shop in stores for a few items
    f. Can be left at home alone
7. Parent cooperation
    a. Are free from general anxiety regarding trainee
    b. Are intelligent and have been consistently following staff suggestions
    c. Have confidence in staff and accept program objectives

    d. Have realistic attitudes toward trainee

    e. Agree with each other on expectations of trainee [pp. 70-71].

In the first section of the travel candidate selection criteria, Cortazzo and Sansone (1969) stated that a client must have an IQ of at least 30 in order to qualify as a candidate for travel instruction. However, the authors soon realized that intelligence test scores were unimportant criteria in the selection process. There is no empirical evidence of any relationship between the score on an intelligence test and the ability to learn independent travel skills. The results of other travel training programs concur with the conclusion that intelligence test scores are not a valid predictor of a client's success or lack of success in independent travel (Tobias, 1963; Kubat, 1973; Laus, 1974).

The next selection criterion was that the client must have "good physical appearance and freedom from ... gross secondary handicaps" (Cortazzo & Sansone, 1969). The secondary handicaps of physical stigmata, epilepsy, orthopedic defects, visual defects, auditory defects, and heart defects do not necessarily prohibit a client from learning independent travel skills. A client's physical stigmata is not a determiner of whether he has skills or ability to learn skills involved in independent travel. The ability to perform a task should not be judged on his appearance. Many persons with epilepsy can function independently on public transportation facilities when their illness is controlled by medication. If a client has an orthopedic defect, modification can be made in his instruction through consultation or auxiliary instruction by a physical therapist. Those clients with visual defects also may require modification of the travel instruction program but should not be dismissed as candidates on the basis of not having a normal visual acuity. Consultation with an orientation and mobility specialist for the visually impaired may provide a valuable resource for travel instruction. Auditory defects also do not affect the learning of travel skills, for one is not required to hear while walking along a sidewalk, crossing a street, or boarding a bus. Those clients with heart defects may be considered as candidates upon approval of a physician. In summary, the existence of a secondary handicap may require modification of instruction but should not necessarily eliminate a client as a candidate for travel instruction.

The third candidate selection criterion, "social maturity," included qualities that may give indications as to the probability of a client to be successful in travel instruction. Independent travel requires a person to be responsible for his actions, dependable in his daily travel, and able to interact in a mature manner with the public. Moreover, the travel instruction process requires that clients reliably follow a set of instructions. If the client demonstrates these qualities in other program areas, this may be one indicator of readiness for travel instruction. If he does not, the client ought not be eliminated as a candidate based on this one criterion. Traveling and the resultant independence may have more internal meaning to the client than previous activities in which he has been a participant. As a result of learning independent travel skills, the client may be able to view himself as having more of an adult function and thus be able to demonstrate a greater maturity. Generally this selection criterion is helpful in identifying candidates.

The fourth selection criterion, "emotional stability," is relevant to predicting success of those clients in travel instruction. A travel candidate cannot be one who panics easily when faced with an unfamiliar situation or behaves irrationally due to phobias, i.e. animals, the dark. A candidate's behavior must be generally free of offensive habits such as genital play; he must not seek attention or be easily led. Furthermore, the candidate must have a fairly high frustration tolerance. These prerequisite behaviors listed by Cortazzo and Sansone seem basic and necessary for successful independent travel.

The behaviors of the fifth candidate selection criterion, "communication skills," are not prerequisites for a client to be an independent traveler. It is not essential to use intelligible speech while traveling. When is it necessary to speak when riding a public bus? The fare is put in the farebox; if the clients wants a transfer, he can communicate this need by pointing a finger to where the transfers are kept. When alighting from the bus, he can ring the buzzer and then walk to the front of the bus. While it would be advantageous for a client to be able to use a public telephone, it is not a critical prerequisite. If the client becomes disoriented, he can be trained to display his personal identification card to a policeman. In general, the skills listed in this section seem inappropriate to choosing a candidate for travel instruction.

The sixth candidate selection criterion, "degree of independence," is quite subjective and cannot predict ability to learn from an intensive, structured program of mobility instruction. The client may not have the opportunity to demonstrate independence due to the low expectations or the overprotection of those adults around him. If he is able to demonstrate independence, it is to his advantage, but this criterion cannot predict ability to learn.

The subpoints of the final selection criterion, "parental cooperation," also are not helpful in choosing candidates. Yes, parental permission is a requirement, but how can one ask that parents be free from anxiety regarding the independent travel of their child? Is the parent's intelligence a criterion? Hopefully they can have confidence in the staff and have realistic attitudes toward the client. But these parental attitudes are not helpful in determining whether or not a client can benefit from travel training.

To summarize, five of the seven candidate selection criteria are not helpful in accurately predicting which clients will be able to be successful in learning independent travel. The candidate selection criteria in the "emotional stability" and "social maturity" sections appear to be helpful in predicting those clients who will not be able to benefit from travel instruction.

### Teaching Identification Fact-Skills

The candidate selection criteria for determining which clients might benefit from travel instruction having been reviewed, the second major phase of Cortazzo and Sansone's travel training program, "Teaching Identification Fact-Skills," (1969) will now be examined. The clients were taught basic facts about themselves, their homes, and the activity center; identification of stationary and moving objects; traffic, street, and safety signs; community helpers; and warning signals (including flashing and red lights, whistles, and sirens). These objects and related items are identified by Cortazzo and Sansone (1969) in the following list:

| *Self* | *Signs* | *Colors* |
|---|---|---|
| Name | Stairs | Red |
| Home address | Caution | Green |
| Phone number | Escalator | Amber |
| Age | Taxi | |
| Parents' names | Push — Pull | *Money* |
| | Press | |
| *Center* | Push to Open | 1¢   Penny |
| | Move to Rear | 5¢   Nickel |
| Name of center | Men | 10¢   Dime |
| Address | Ladies | 25¢   Quarter |
| Phone number | Women | 50¢   Half-dollar |
| Director or | Restroom | $1.00 Dollar |
| instructor's name | Danger | |
| | High Voltage | *Numbers* |
| *Signs* | Keep Out | |
| | Shelter | 1 through 25 |
| Stop — Red | No Smoking | |
| Go — Green | Emergency Door | *Police signals* |
| Walk — Green | Take Cover | |
| Don't Walk — Red | Men Working | To cross |
| Cross | Explosives | To stop |
| Bus Stop | Detour | Right |
| Train Station | Use Other Door | Left |
| Downtown | Use Other Exit | Middle |
| Uptown | Closed | |
| Local | Police | *Weather (Radio & TV)* |
| Entrance | Conductor | |
| Exit | Tokens | Threatening |
| Change | Safety Zone | Rain, Snow, Fog |
| Information | Crossing | Temperatures |
| Tickets | | |
| Telephone | *Warning Signals* | *Time* |
| Deposit Money | | |
| Fare 15¢, etc. | Sirens | Morning |
| In — Out | Whistles | Noon |
| Up — Down | Flashing lights | Afternoon |
| | | Evening |
| | | Night |
| | | Hour — Half-hour |
| | | [p. 72]. |

The authors stated that the best way to teach identification facts was to take the client out in the community to identify actual signs, colors, and objects in conjunction with "classroom-type" instruction. After some progress was made, parents were asked to walk the clients in the community to identify signs, colors, and objects. The preceding list is a useful guide of facts that a traveler might need to know in order to travel independently in the community. However, there is no indication of any sequence in which they are to be learned. Is knowledge of these facts required for independent travel? Are there a few that must be mastered in order to travel independently? Are some optional? Should they be included in an on-going curriculum beginning at an early age?

In this second major phase of their travel training program, Cortazzo and Sansone (1969) also describe teaching the use of a two-sided identification card to clients who are not able to communicate verbally. One side is colored red and is used by the client enroute home; the reverse side, used enroute to the center is green. Each side states in capital letters the phrase "PLEASE HELP ME LOCATE THE FOLLOWING." Under this heading, the appropriate person's name, home or center's name, and the required conveyances are listed. The authors stated, "Because it was essential for the trainee to learn how to rely on the ID card, all were asked to present the card many times during the day." Why is it essential for the client to rely on the ID card? Use of an ID card is not a tool of independence but a sign or symbol of the client's dependence on others for help. It communicates to the community as well as to the client that he is different, retarded, and dependent on others. If the client is familiar with his travel route as a result of travel training, there is no need to seek assistance en route to his destination.

## Teaching Pedestrian Techniques

The third major phase involved teaching the client such basic conventions for pedestrian travel as keeping to the right on the sidewalks, crossing at corners, and obeying traffic lights and safety signs. Clients learned basic techniques in street crossing and boarding a public conveyance as well as selecting apparel appropriate to the daily weather conditions. These skills seem to be basic and necessary for independent travel.

## Teaching the Travel Route

After confidence was gained in the previous areas, Cortazzo and Sansone (1969) reported that mastery of the specific travel route to and from the center was the fourth major instructional phase. With the help of parents, the simplest and most direct route was chosen. Initially, the instructor took the client through the complete route several times. The route was then broken down into what were considered manageable units; the authors stated that the complexity of the unit and the client's ability determined what constituted a manageable unit. A unit usually took no longer than a maximum of two weeks to learn and was mastered in sequence. Each learned unit was traveled every day, which resulted in overlearning. When all of the units were mastered, the instructor would allow the client to lead him through the complete route.

The final evaluation was made when the client completed the trip alone, while the instructor followed without being seen. In this manner, the client demonstrated his learned travel skills, confidence, and poise under real conditions. The authors reported that the client was teamed up with other travel clients who used the same route. The average time period to learn a route was about one and one-half months (Cortazzo and Sansone, 1969).

Although Cortazzo and Sansone used a manageable unit organization for teaching the travel route, the instructional process may be more efficient and meaningful to the client if the entire route is traveled during each daily lesson. The client will more clearly see the importance and result of each step of the route; the total trip experienced by the client can provide a complete perspective of what is being demanded of him.

Furthermore, the practice of teaming up a client who has

demonstrated competency in traveling with other independent travelers using the same route is a questionable one. In contrast to this procedure, it may be advisable to discourage joint travel of clients. The danger is that clients may learn to rely on others and not on their own newly learned travel skills.

## Teaching the Handling of Money

The fifth major phase of travel instruction as delineated by Cortazzo and Sansone was the "teaching of handling of money." The authors stated that this proved to be a difficult training area, for money had little meaning or significance to most clients. It was necessary to teach money skills daily, and to reinforce these skills during the daily processes of the centers because clients had to pay bus fares daily. Cortazzo and Sansone (1969) stated that:

> The lunch program, dining out, and other activities requiring money all placed added meaning and emphasis on learning the money concept.
>
> The introduction of subcontract work resulted in even the lowest functioning trainee looking forward to pay day [p. 7].

Use of money to pay the fare of a public conveyance is an important part of independent travel. However, the teaching of money skills for independent travel may not be necessary in teaching independent travel skills. In many cities, all that is required when boarding a public conveyance is to display a prepaid weekly or monthly pass. Many citizens use this method for paying fares because it is a less expensive and a more convenient method of payment. Thus clients can be encouraged to buy prepaid passes as other citizens do, save money, and at the same time not be required to always have the exact change.

## Teaching Conveyance Identification

"Conveyance identification" was listed by Cortazzo and Sansone (1969) as the sixth major phase in teaching independent travel. They stated that many times identification of the conveyance was made by numbers or colors, and often it was necessary to learn the words of street destinations marked on the vehicle. The authors (1969) stated:

> Initially, the trainees and the instructor would stand at the bus stop or train station and wait for the vehicle. The instructor carried flash cards and drilled the trainees in between conveyance arrivals. The card contained scaled down drawings of the front of the vehicle and, where necessary, the boarding side, along with the appropriate cues. The trainees were given pocket and pocketbook-size flash cards. In cases where the cues could not be memorized, cards were used as a crutch in identifying the correct conveyance [p. 77].

Conveyance identification is a critical skill that must be mastered to maintain orientation. The above methods for teaching conveyance identification are appropriate.

## Parent Counseling

"Parent counseling" was cited by Cortazzo and Sansone (1969) as the seventh major phase of their travel training program. They listed the steps in the parent counseling program as follows:

1. Evaluation of parents, including estimated potential for accepting the travel training
2. Review of trainee's progress in the activity program, both in the center and in the home
3. Discussion of trainee's potential, including observation of other travel trainees with similar potential
4. Discussion and acceptance of evaluation as the first unit in the travel training program
5. Discussion of results of evaluation, e.g. how much trainee knows, how much progress he made, how he compares to others who have completed the program, etc.
6. Selection of the conveyances and safest route, and a discussion of possible problems
7. Selection of a staff person in whom parents have confidence, and assurance that safeguards for the trainee will be maintained
8. Discussion of the second unit of travel training

9. Discussion of trainee's progress — utilizing charts and graphs for comparison to other trainees and having trainee demonstrate what he has learned before parents
10. Assignments to parents so that they may become actively involved
11. Demonstration of independent travel after full discussion of how well the trainee has mastered all the required skills
12. Presentation of travel training certificate to the trainee for successful completion of the course — made at a special meeting of parents, staff, and trainees [pp. 78-80].

The preceding outline is a comprehensive guide to the process of parental counseling and can aid in the parental acceptance of the travel training program.

In summary, Cortazzo and Sansone (1969) cited outcomes of the travel training program:

> Successful trainees demonstrated a great deal of concomitant improvement in many personal, social and economic skills. For many trainees the ability to travel ended their isolated restriction to their homes, and their parents developed more positive attitudes toward them [p. 81].

The factors that contributed to failure of clients to learn independent travel were primarily "emotional instability, social immaturity, and parental overprotection." One center reported that their travel budget was reduced from $21,000 to $10,000 in three years as a result of a successful travel training program.

## THE KUBAT PROGRAM

In 1973, another successful travel training program for mentally retarded persons was reported by Kubat. The site of this program was the Columbus Community Center in Salt Lake City, Utah. At this center, the author stated that "mentally retarded and physically handicapped adults [were] trained in academics, a sheltered workshop, and a skilled training center." Realizing that 90 percent of the clients relied on chartered bus or parents to transport them daily to the center, it was decided to implement a travel training program. Kubat (1973) stated that:

> Any agency which serves a handicapped population, and has
> as one of its goals the adjustment of its clients to the outside
> community, must consider the problem of independent travel.
> For example, clients may have problems with transportation
> to and from the agency, places of special training, or job
> interviews and job application.
>
> This situation produced special disadvantages for individ-
> uals in the sheltered workshop or skilled training program
> since use of the chartered bus meant arriving late, leaving
> early, and consequently missing several hours of valuable
> training each day. Also, the use of chartered school buses
> perpetuated a school atmosphere at the Center which de-
> tracted from preparing the client to take jobs in the commu-
> nity [p. 36].

The study reported the success of thirteen clients in learning
to travel independently to and from the Center. The clients had
mental ages from six to twelve, with IQs in the educable and
trainable range (Kubat, 1973). The clients in other reported
programs were limited to those in the trainable range (Tobias,
1963; Cortazzo & Sansone, 1969). Thus, Kubat's clients were on
a somewhat higher intellectual level. There was no further
description of the clients who participated in the travel training
program. Kubat (1973) listed four different phases of the travel
training program:

> First, the trainee and staff member discussed appropriate bus
> riding behavior; second, the trainee was shown his bus route
> in one of the Center's vehicles; third, a bus ride was simulated
> in the same vehicle; and fourth, the trainee rode the city bus
> with a staff member [p. 37].

Each of these four phases is summarized and critically reviewed
in the following section.

## Instruction of Appropriate Bus Riding Behaviors

The first phase of instruction according to Kubat was the
"instruction of appropriate bus riding behaviors."

During an interview a staff member explained each aspect of

correct bus riding behavior, asked the trainee questions about
the important points, and answered any questions the trainee
had about the program [p. 37].

Kubat stated that a staff member conducted the interview, but
he did not give a clear description of the instructor. Is he a
professional? Is this one person assigned to a client until he
becomes a competent independent traveler? While Kubat stated
that the instructor discussed appropriate bus riding behavior
with the client, he did not indicate that the staff member and
client actually rode a public bus. Traveling en route with the
client would have provided the perfect setting for an explanation of and question-and-answer session on bus riding behavior. More importantly, the instructor would have been a
positive model for appropriate bus riding behavior.

### Route Familiarization

The second phase of travel instruction, "route familiarization," is next described by Kubat (1973):

One of the Center's vehicles ... was used to drive the trainee
along his bus route and show him major reference points
such as large buildings, parks, and construction sites. Each
trainee was taught to use a specific reference point so he
could remember when he should pull the buzzer cord to indicate that he wanted to exit [p. 37].

Using a Center vehicle is a questionable technique for familiar-
izing a client with a public bus route. A more meaningful and
realistic method would be to use an actual public bus. If the
client is accompanied on the public bus by his instructor, the
objectives of familiarization can be attained in the real setting.

During this "route familiarization" Kubat (1973) stated:

The bus route itself was simplified by dividing it into small
segments. Thus the trainee was prompted to remember the
number of turns the bus would make from the time he
boarded until the time he should exit, the placement and
numbering of street signs along the route were noted, the
streets at the end of each bus ride were pointed out, and
physical reference points were located along each segment of

the route [p. 37].

The memorization of the number of bus turns, the placement and numbering of street signs and street names seems to be an onerous and useless task to demand. It would seem more efficient to ask a client to recall physical reference points along the route and one specific point where he alights from the bus.

## Simulation of the Bus Ride

The third phase of travel instruction as described by Kubat was the "simulation of the bus ride" (1973). Again, might it not be more meaningful to spend time riding the actual bus rather than simulating this experience? Spending more instruction time in the real situation would provide the opportunity for unexpected situations to occur, and the clients would have the supervision of the instructor to help in dealing with these situations. The bus might be overly crowded, an unruly passenger might be present, or the bus might deviate from its usual route. By having as many experiences as possible in the real situation, the client would thus be better prepared for unexpected situations when he would begin to travel alone.

## Riding the Bus

The final phase, "riding the bus," as described by Kubat, was the terminal experience whereby the trainee demonstrated his travel competence (1973). There was no prompting by the instructor, and if the trainee was not able to demonstrate competence, retraining in the Center's vehicle was deemed necessary.

The author summarized his article by stating that (1973):

It might be conjectured that such a successful experience would affect each individual's concept of his own learning abilities, the manner in which he deals with future problems, and even perhaps how he relates to his general environment.

In conclusion, it is hoped that the overall result of training the individual to use the city transit system will be to speed their progress toward becoming more effective functioning members of the community [p. 42].

## THE NEW YORK CITY PUBLIC SCHOOLS PROGRAM

In 1973, Margaret-M. Groce authored a funding evaluation report of the travel training for the handicapped program in the New York City Public Schools. Groce stated:

> The travel training program for the funding year 1972-73 was designed to train handicapped youngsters between the ages of 16-21 to travel independently to an Occupational Training Center or other pre-vocational or vocational training facilities. Specific objectives were:
> 1. To screen approximately 300 educable and trainable mentally retarded youngsters and evaluate their ability to travel independently.
> 2. To screen approximately 100 brain injured youngsters and evaluate their ability to travel independently.
> 3. To train approximately 200 educable and trainable mentally retarded youngsters and 75 brain injured youngsters to use the complex New York City transit system as a prerequisite to vocational training and future employment; in particular, to train to travel independently to an Occupational Training Center or other vocational training facilities.
> 4. To provide parent education to foster positive attitudes toward travel.
> 5. To provide teacher training in travel training methods to teachers of the mentally retarded and the brain injured.
> 6. To develop curriculum materials applicable to vocational skills [p. 1].

In order to attain these objectives, the activities and instructional content included a screening process to identify candidates for training, the development of curriculum materials for classroom teachers, in-service training of classroom teachers to inform them of the techniques used in travel training, direct individual and small group training experiences, parent workshops and interviews, in-service training for the travel training staff, and instruction of travel-related skills in the classroom (Groce, 1973).

The daily travel instruction was implemented by a trained paraprofessional under the supervision of a professional.

Trainees received individualized instruction and the program was designed to teach the following (Groce, 1973):

1. The safest and most direct route from home to the vocational or prevocational training facility and back.
2. Procedures to follow if lost or confused during travel.
3. Appropriate behavior in public vehicles.
4. Use of the telephones.
5. Special procedures for trainees with epilepsy.

During the 1972-73 school year, Groce cited the following outcomes of the travel training program:

1. One hundred ninety-nine (199) mentally retarded youngsters between the ages of 16-21 learned to travel independently to an Occupational Training Center.
2. Ten (10) mentally retarded trainees entered a sheltered workshop because of learning to travel independently.
3. Twenty-two (22) mentally retarded youngsters already in the Occupational Training Centers were trained to travel independently.
4. Twelve (12) brain injured youngsters in public schools and ten (10) youngsters on homebound instruction learned to travel independently.
5. Five (5) youngsters from the School for the Hearing and Language Impaired, two (2) youngsters from the School for the Deaf, and one (1) visually handicapped youngster were trained to travel independently.
6. Four hundred four (404) parents who were contacted by the travel training staff participated in parent workshops or individual interviews [pp. 2-3].

The program of travel training for the handicapped in the New York City Public Schools is a large and apparently successful program in a massive and complex city. While there is no published description of this program, its breadth and scope warrant mention in this text.

## THE LAUS PROGRAM

In 1974, I reported the success of a program in the Pittsburgh

Public School system that, in its first year, resulted in thirty-five pupils learning to travel independently via the public transit between home and school. The success of this program and the response to the journal article has provided the impetus for writing this book. The remainder of this work delineates the program for travel instruction that I first reported in 1974.

## CONCLUSIONS

The preceding review of literature indicates that when many cognitively impaired persons are given an appropriate instructional program, they are able to learn independent travel skills. In the past, handicapped persons have not been expected to travel independently, and consequently they have not been capable of doing so. The travel instruction programs of Tobias (1963), Cortazzo and Sansone (1969), Kubat (1973), Groce (1973), and Laus (1974) have raised expectations for cognitively impaired persons and as a result have raised their performance.

It becomes clear that the teaching of independent travel skills is vital to the process of reducing dependence of handicapped persons. Formal programs to teach independent travel skills must become an integral part of the curriculum in public schools, postschool activity centers, sheltered workshops, group homes, and state institutions serving handicapped persons. The specific skills learned through instruction of independent travel are basic and necessary for the achievement of long-term goals for handicapped persons. Similar to orientation and mobility programs serving blind persons, professionals concerned with the normalization of all handicapped persons must implement specialized programs that teach independent travel skills.

Chapter 2

# IN THE BEGINNING

> Here is Edward Bear, coming downstairs now, bump, bump, bump, on the back of his head, behind Christopher Robin. It is, as far as he knows, the only way of coming downstairs, but sometimes he feels that there really is another way, if only he could stop bumping for a moment and think of it.
>
> A. A. Milne
> *Winnie-The-Pooh*

FOR many years, the program for trainable mentally retarded pupils in the Pittsburgh Public Schools, like Edward Bear, had been bumping down the stairs on its head. While bumping, somehow we believed that there really could be another way. The Pennsylvania Right to Education Act of 1971 provided the opportunity to "stop bumping for a moment and think of it." Many positive outcomes resulted from this "moment" to think, but the one that provides the focus of this book is the development of an innovative program to teach travel skills to sighted trainable mentally retarded pupils.

This chapter discusses the establishment of this program: the setting, the risk, the basic goal, and the aspects of travel instruction programs for the blind that were adapted to provide the beginning framework for the implementation of this program. First, the pupils and the setting are described in order for the reader to gain a perspective of how and why travel instruction plays a vital role in the habilitation process for impaired citizens. Second, the risk involved in such a training process is discussed because it is inherent in the commitment to implement a travel instruction program. Third, the basic goal of the travel instruction program is delineated in order to outline the direction of this book for the reader. Finally, a model for the

25

establishment of the instructional process is described; it is based on one modified from existing instructional programs that teach independent travel skills to blind persons.

## THE SETTING

Pittsburgh Public School pupils who perform in the 25 to 50 IQ range on intelligence tests administered by school psychologists are labeled as trainable mentally retarded. While the primary disability of these pupils is considered to be trainable mental retardation, a number have the following additional secondary handicaps: brain injury, emotional disturbance, deafness, and physical handicap. All these pupils, whose chronological ages range between five and twenty-one, attend one large, centrally located facility in this urban school system.

This facility, referred to as a *center* to differentiate it from traditional school connotations, is designed to meet the educational, life-adjustment, and vocational needs of its four hundred pupils. Basic academic skills are taught to pupils according to their presently diagnosed functioning ability. Many of these skills, e.g. number skills, word identification, etc., are related to future life adjustment and vocational needs. In teaching life adjustment skills, the center endeavors to teach such necessary daily living skills such as grooming, dressing, basic food preparation, and home maintenance. An important part of the center's program deals with the teaching of work attitudes and skills that are necessary for future adjustment to work settings; these settings may be sheltered workshops or competitive employment. The expectations of the center are that pupils will eventually participate in some type of work setting.

To understand the context whereby travel instruction became an integral element of the program, the vocational training program, the key aspect of the center's habilitative process, needs further elucidation. This program was developed by Ronald C. Conant following extensive research and staff development and was based on the many articles and practices of Mr. Simon Olshansky, the Executive Director of the Community Workshops, Inc., in Boston (Conant, 1976). The training program utilizes a workshop approach with normalization principles and provides vocational evaluation, work-adjustment training, and job training with suitable job placement. It provides referral for appropriate services for the population such as dental and medical services, counseling for the pupils and parents, and social programming.

In order to reflect the normalization philosophy within the vocational training program, the assumptions of the staff include (Conant, 1976):

> natural drive toward independence and normality; self direction and self determination; raised expectations result in raised performance; avoidance of labeling; growth and development occur best in natural settings; application, experience, doing; and opportunity motivates.

Conant states that these assumptions are found in the workshop practices as (1976):

> current medical information; calling the student 'worker;' modeling staff behavior; teaching staff are considered supervisors and bosses; regularly raising the work expectations; decision making power; time out procedures; positive reinforcement and modest financial reinforcer; work that is realistic and varied in kind and complexity; providing normal incentives; weekly staff meetings to insure staff cohesion and communication; and ongoing staff inservices.

There are five major training areas in the vocational training program (Conant, 1976). First, the assembly/clerical department provides work experience in light benchwork including assembly, sorting, counting, clerical reproduction in machine operation (ditto, mimeograph, photocopy, etc.), stapling, collating, quality control, and packaging. Second, the food service department provides experiences centered in the cafeteria that teach skills in food preparation, service, busing, operation of industrial dishwashers, sweeping and general cleanup, and cashiering. Third, the industrial production department provides experience in use of handtools and machine operation performed on an assembly-line basis. Fourth, the industrial maintenance department provides experiences and teaches skills in general maintenance and custodial tasks. Finally, the activities of daily living program, which is centered in a model apartment, teaches personal and self-care skills on both an individual and a group basis. Teacher and parent consultation is also provided.

By including a wide range of vocational experiences, the main emphasis of the center's programming is to provide the pupils with vocational skills to permit them to successfully adjust to a post-school vocational setting. But there is another set of key skills required for vocational adjustment; these are the skills involved in being able to travel independently to a work setting.

Prior to 1972, the Pittsburgh Public Schools transported all trainable mentally retarded pupils to the center by leased vans, taxis, and school buses. The Division for Exceptional Children of this school district made no attempt to train pupils to travel independently; it did not expect adolescent pupils to travel alone on public transportation facilities. With the wisdom of hindsight, it now seems inconsistent for any program to teach work skills without ever dealing with the question of how pupils would travel to work. The staff lacked the expectations and the pupils lacked the capability. This was the situation in Pittsburgh Public Schools then, and it remains the situation in most other programs for handicapped persons today.

## THE RISK

Unlike many other public school divisions for exceptional children, the one in Pittsburgh undertook the considerable risk of trying a new program. The Director of the Division, Doctor Ruth L. Scott, believed that if blind persons could learn independent travel skills as a result of a specialized instructional program, then mentally retarded persons who possess normal vision could also learn to travel independently if a specialized instructional program could be developed to meet their particular needs. Inherent in such a plan was a considerable amount of risk. Were parents, teachers, and the community prepared for such an undertaking? Could such a training program result in bodily harm to pupils? Might pupils become lost in the city? Would pupils be ridiculed while using the public transit? On the other hand, would we be depriving pupils of needed skills by not providing an opportunity for independent travel? Would we be stifling the potential growth and independence for our retarded pupils? Were we being overprotective and did we have low expectations for our pupils? These were some of the questions we had to ask ourselves and openly discuss during the planning process. We opted for the risk.

In agreement with Robert Perske, we decided to permit our pupils to have the opportunity for risk taking (1972). He explains:

> Many who work with the handicapped, impaired, disadvantaged, and aged tend to be overzealous in their attempts to 'protect,' 'comfort,' 'keep safe,' 'take care,' and 'watch.' Acting on these impulses at the right time can be benevolent, helpful, and developmental. But, if they are acted upon exclusively or excessively, without allowing for each client's individuality and growth potential, they will overprotect and emotionally smother the intended beneficiary. In fact, such overprotection endangers the client's human dignity, and tends to keep him from experiencing the risk taking of ordinary life which is necessary for normal human growth and development [p. 195].

Inherent in the orientation and mobility program is risk. But prudent risk will provide the opportunity for pupil growth. As Perske (1972) aptly says, "to deny any person their fair share of risk taking experiences is to further cripple them for healthy living [p. 199]."

## THE BASIC GOAL

In September, 1972, the Division for Exceptional Children established a position for an orientation and mobility instructor to teach travel skills to its population of sighted trainable mentally retarded pupils. It had become clear that we had to try to teach this set of skills to as many pupils as possible, if it were possible at all. I was hired to design and implement this program. My dual certification and experience in working with blind clients and mentally retarded ones and my commitment to this task, coupled with the confidence that it is possible, helped me to get the job.

The long-range goal was that many of our pupils would learn to be able to travel independently in the community as adults. In order to help facilitate the achievement of this competency, the basic goal of our program was to teach pupils to use the public transit system to travel independently to and from the center in lieu of taxicabs and vans. Each pupil received instruction for his particular route. There was no attempt to teach alternate routes or routes to other destinations. The rationale for this approach was that by teaching one route, the pupils would learn the necessary travel skills that could be generalized for use to future destinations. In addition, they would learn to be comfortable with the use of public transit facilities, develop confidence in interacting with the public, and feel they were succeeding in the performance of a normal adult function.

## THE BLIND LEAD THE WAY FOR THE RETARDED

In the conceptualization of such a program, my initial step was to apply the expertise and experience of orientation and mobility programs for the blind to the special needs of our sighted trainable mentally retarded pupils. Richard Welsh, an orientation and mobility instructor for the blind, supported my belief that orientation and mobility programs for the blind can provide a framework that might be modified by other disability groups such as the mentally retarded (1972):

> The expertise and the experience of mobility instructors for the visually handicapped are relevant to rehabilitation and education programs for other handicapped groups. Mobility instructors should reach out to these other programs and share their past successes and difficulties in teaching visually handicapped clients to travel independently ... much of what has been done for the visually handicapped can be adapted for other groups to aid their independent travel [p. 109].

With these ideas in mind, I decided to incorporate four basic aspects of existing orientation and mobility programs for the blind for use in establishing the basis of my program to teach independent travel skills to our sighted trainable mentally retarded pupils. These four aspects include (1) terminology, (2) the specialist role, (3) a one-to-one ratio of instructor and pupil, and (4) orientation and mobility instruction taking place in the real setting. A more detailed explanation of these four aspects follows.

First, the term *orientation and mobility instruction* replaced the term *travel training,* which had been used in previous studies with the mentally retarded. There were two reasons for being careful about the terminology. The former was a more explicit descriptor, for it more adequately described maintenance of orientation along with movement (Laus, 1974). As Ball (1964) stated:

> Orientation ... is a dynamic process, inherent in the total mobility function, for as the person moves, his surroundings are constantly changing and he has to keep up with them. Mobility, then, is not only being able to move but being able to establish and maintain contact with the significant realities of the environment as well [p. 110].

Independent travel is not only the physical act of moving but also involves a person's awareness of his surroundings as he relates to everyday living (Laus, 1974). In addition to this argument, I believe that the term *orientation and mobility instruction* should have supplanted that of *travel training* because the former would take on more of a generic connotation than the latter. Orientation and mobility instruction should not be limited to instruction of blind persons but should be perceived as the instruction of all persons who require a formalized learning experience to acquire independent travel skills. For these reasons the term *orientation and mobility instruction* came to be a part of the vocabulary of the Division for Exceptional Children in the Pittsburgh Public Schools and is used throughout this book.

The establishment of a specialist role for the orientation and mobility instructor was the second aspect of orientation and mobility programs for the blind that I adapted for use with the sighted mentally retarded. As orientation and mobility instructors became specialists in teaching blind persons independent travel skills, it seemed imperative for a specialist to teach sighted trainable mentally retarded pupils to travel independently. The instruction of orientation and mobility skills is a full-time role in any program for mentally retarded persons. Other published programs indicated that assorted staff members were assigned the task of teaching travel skills. In these programs, it seemed that whoever was free at the moment was recruited for travel instruction. As in the field of blindness, I contend that the orientation and mobility instructor should be trained professional, or paraprofessional under supervision of a professional, with expertise to deal with the travel needs of mentally retarded persons. Admittedly, much of the instruction involves repetitious travel experiences. However, the instructor must make critical judgments in providing meaningful learning experiences and evaluating whether a pupil has demonstrated competence to be permitted to travel alone in the community. These critical judgments require background, knowledge, experience, and maturity not easily gained by any staff member who happens to be free at the moment. Mistakes of judgment could result in serious physical, social, or emotional harm to the pupils or could result in misguided pressure to terminate a much-needed and successful program.

Third, the program insisted on a one-to-one teaching ratio of instructor and pupil. As I stated in my earlier article (Laus, 1974):

> Because of the pupils' limited ability, necessity for repetition
> in learning, concern for pupil safety, it was imperative that a
> one-to-one instructor-pupil ratio exist for orientation and
> mobility instruction [p. 71].

Each pupil required an individual travel route from his home to school, and this required an individualized instructional program. Each pupil had individual strengths, needs, and handicaps which required important adjustments of the program. If more than one pupil were given instruction at a time, it would be difficult to assess the independent progress of the individual pupil. The skills eventually had to be demonstrated by each pupil alone. In group teaching, pupils might tend to rely on other pupils for movement cues within the travel process. Thus, as in orientation and mobility instruction for the blind, the one-to-one instructor-pupil ratio was vital to the success of my program.

The fourth concept that I utilized for my program was that orientation and mobility instruction should take place in the real setting. Orientation and mobility instruction for the blind takes place in the real setting, for significant learning can only occur when the learner actually interacts with his environment. Very little can be learned about the real world through simulation in controlled settings. Thus, the same must be true in regard to an orientation and mobility program for mentally retarded persons. I question the practice of some published programs that report use of mock buses and other simulation activities. As in programs for the blind, my view was that real learning must occur only in the real setting. While some component skills can be learned through classroom experiences and simulation, the retarded pupil should have the opportunity to have as many instructional experiences as possible in the community on regular public transit facilities.

These four aspects of orientation and mobility for the blind were modified in establishing an orientation and mobility program for the trainable mentally retarded pupils in the Pittsburgh Public Schools. The next step was to begin to identify candidates for instruction.

Chapter 3

# THE IDENTIFICATION ────────────
# OF CANDIDATES ────────────

When a person is perceived as deviant, he is cast into a role that carries with it powerful expectancies. Strangely enough, these expectancies not only take hold of the mind of the perceiver, but of the perceived person as well. It is a well established fact that a person's behavior tends to be profoundly affected by the role expectations that are placed upon him. Generally, people will play the roles they have been assigned. This permits those who define social roles to make self-fulfilling prophecies by predicting that someone cast into a certain role will emit behavior consistent with that role. Unfortunately, role-appropriate behavior will then often be interpreted to be a person's 'natural' mode of acting, rather than a mode elicited by environmental events and circumstances.

Wolf Wolfensberger
*The Principle of Normalization in Human Services*

**T**HERE has been no research or development of formal measures to help identify candidates who can benefit from independent travel instruction. IQ scores are not adequate indicators. Tobias stated that those mentally retarded persons with IQs on the higher end of the continuum are more likely to benefit from travel instruction (1963). While this may be true, this finding was of little value to me because it did not measure probable success nor give any indication as to how a person could be identified as a candidate. Intelligence test scores might give some indications as to what potential a person might reach academically, but these test scores cannot predict whether or not a person will benefit from orientation and mobility instruction. Factors other than intelligence enter into achievement of independent travel. Such factors include social emotional readiness and the ability to initiate movement and to make action decisions. The use of traditional intelligence test scores as a basis for identifying candidates is difficult to justify. Although it is obvious that intelligence at some point is related to the need for this training, the factors measured on traditional IQ tests do not seem to be relevant; they are nonspecific. Many more factors must be considered. A more rational approach appears to be a careful identification of the specific skills necessary for success in independent travel followed by an assessment of each pupil's potential for acquiring these skills.

While I had a conceptualization of what characteristics were required of travel candidates, it was difficult to establish workable criteria to determine which mentally retarded persons were capable of benefiting from orientation and mobility instruction. Observations of pupils made it apparent that many did not have the attending ability, emotional stability, and basic academic skills necessary to travel independently. Yet I had to make a judgment, and it had to be correct in almost every case. This was especially true when the program was new and unproven; the program had to be safe as well as feasible. In order to establish the feasibility of the program, initially I was forced to exclude some pupils who might succeed in order to be sure that all who entered orientation and mobility instruction succeeded. Once the program matured and demonstrated success, I was then able to risk training some pupils who might fail in order to reach all pupils who may succeed.

## FOUR REQUISITES FOR CANDIDACY

In looking at pupils to determine who should be considered as candidates for orientation and mobility instruction, I established four basic requirements. Candidates should: (1) demonstrate social emotional readiness, (2) be able to learn basic routines, (3) be able to distinguish a particular bus from a set of others, and (4) be able to make action decisions and to initiate movement. These requirements were initially nebulous, and they may still seem so to the reader. It was a difficult task to specify the requisite behaviors which demonstrate success in each category. To clarify this process I examined the specific situations faced by a public bus rider and outlined the decisions that a pupil would have to make.

First, a candidate must be able to deal and interact appropriately with unfamiliar people and situations. The pupil will be required to encounter an entirely new milieu in his daily travel to school. A pupil might have to deal with various personalities. He might be faced with inconsiderate stares of other bus riders, with Good Samaritan types who wish to provide needless assistance, with panhandlers asking for a spare quarter, with the teasing of young adolescents, with a friendly wino, or with a gregarious grandmother whose best friend has a retarded child and therefore is an expert in mental retardation. Some examples of unfamiliar situations a pupil might encounter include an overcrowded bus, a high-humidity situation where the windows of the bus become steamed so that the pupil cannot maintain orientation, the bus being detoured, the bus having a mechanical breakdown, or any combination of the above. While some of these encounters with people or unfamiliar situations may not be new to some pupils, they will still be required to deal with them alone, without the support of teachers or family. These situations and combinations of situations do occur while using the public transit, and the pupil should have a relatively high stress tolerance in order for him to deal with these situations without its affecting his judgment processes.

Second, a candidate must be capable of responding consistently to designated stimuli and thereby learn basic routines. A pupil in orientation and mobility instruction will be required to learn a travel route that involves a chain of behaviors composed of stimulus-response units. In order to maintain orientation, the pupil must learn to respond consistently to designated stimuli. For example, a pupil is required to respond to the designated stimulus of a landmark in order to alight from a bus at the proper location. If the pupil becomes distracted from this task or falls asleep, the public bus will pass his point of alightment and the pupil will become disoriented.

Third, a pupil must be capable of discriminating "his" bus

from a set of others that may load at his stop. In Pittsburgh, the public buses are numbered; thus, the pupil is required to discriminate specific numerals from a large set of numerals. This does not mean that pupils are required to identify numerals, know the value of numerals, or to perceive them in any order; the only requirement is that a candidate be capable of knowing the difference between numerals that identify his bus and numerals that do not.

Fourth, the pupil must be able to self-initiate routines and skills that have been learned. Pupils should give indications of being able to initiate movement and behavior on their own without reliance on others for direction. When the pupil is required to respond to visual cues to make a decision to alight from a bus, he must be able to initiate the appropriate response. This means that without prompting, the pupil must perform movements that will result in his alighting at the proper location. If the pupil is required to identify "his" bus, he not only has to identify it, but he must act on his own to move toward it and board the bus before it pulls away.

This requisite behavior is difficult to evaluate. Many of the pupils that I have observed seem to be quite dependent on direction from adults. There seems to be little opportunity for retarded pupils to make decisions and initiate their own movement. The following analogy may be appropriate. I have been driven numerous times to a friend's house that is many miles away. During these trips as a passenger, I never had to make any decisions as to how to reach our destination. I just sat there, listened to the radio, and enjoyed the scenery. Although I had been there many times, when I had to drive myself I couldn't remember the route. In the same way, mentally retarded persons have been in the "passenger seat" all their lives; they just sit there, listen to the music of mainstream life, and enjoy the scenery. There are few opportunities to be in "the driver's seat."

While these four sets of skills give indications of a pupil's readiness for orientation and mobility instruction, a question remains. How can these skills be evaluated to determine if a particular pupil can be considered for orientation and mobility instruction? Obviously, this diagnostic process is the first key to successful implementation of the program.

## INPUT FOR THE ASSESSMENT OF CANDIDATES

A variety of input was assessed to make a judgement as to whether individual pupils possessed or could learn the above four requisite sets of skills. Somehow this information had to then result in a decision. The input came from the following sources: (1) the classroom teachers, (2) the school specialists, (3) the workshop supervisor, and (4) personal observations in classrooms and interaction with pupils.

The teachers, school specialists, and workshop supervisor provided valuable information regarding a pupil's social emotional readiness, academic skills, ability to make action decisions and initiate movement, and the home environment. The following preorientation and mobility survey form was provided to these staff members to compile pertinent information.

## ORIENTATION AND MOBILITY INFORMATION SURVEY

Name _____ Age_____

Address_____

Room No. _____ IQ _____ No. of Siblings _____

Hearing Impairments_____ Vision Impairments _____

Speech Impairments _____

Other Physical Impairments _____

Medical Impairments _____

1. Does pupil get along with his peers? _____
2. Does pupil get along with familiar adults? _____
3. Does pupil get along with unfamiliar adults? _____
4. Does pupil deal appropriately with new and unexpected situations? _____
   _____
5. Does pupil exhibit any bizarre behaviorisms? _____
6. How long of a time period can pupil attend to a task in a group setting? _____

7. How long can the pupil attend to a task in a one-to-one situation? _____

8. Does pupil follow directions? _____

9. Can you rely on pupil to complete a task once it is begun? _____

10. Is pupil able to identify and distinguish green, yellow, and red? _____

11. Is pupil able to identify and distinguish green, yellow, and red signals of a traffic light? _____

12. Is pupil able to count objects? _____

13. Can pupil recognize numerals? _____

14. Is pupil able to identify money? _____

15. Is pupil able to exchange money accurately? _____

16. Can pupil read basic street signs? _____

17. Is pupil able to speak coherently? _____

18. Is pupil able to communicate orally his or her home address and phone number? _____

19. Is pupil able to use a public pay phone independently?

20. Does pupil initiate conversation, or does he only respond once he is addressed? _____

21. Does pupil initiate movement within classroom or building or does he wait for direction? _____

22. Does pupil have to be told to do everything? _____

Remarks _____
_____
_____
_____
_____
_____

The information concerning existence of secondary impairments was important to determine candidacy and to plan for instruction. The only way it would directly affect candidacy was in cases of medical disability where a physician did not give approval. The speech and hearing specialists or the nurse provided this information if applicable. In regards to emotional stability and personality, the teacher commented in questions 1 through 5 how particular pupils dealt with stress and on new and unexpected situations that would occur in the classroom or on field trips. Teachers provided information in questions 6 through 9 concerning the attending behavior of pupils in various situations. Questions 10 through 19 provided information regarding pupils' academic skills. In one case, a pupil was unable to distinguish green, yellow, and red colors. Soon it was discovered that the pupil was color blind, and thus modifications were made in her instructional program. In questions 20 through 22, teachers commented on pupils' ability to make action decisions and initiate movement. The pre-orientation and mobility information survey form helped organize data provided by classroom teachers and school specialists.

In conjunction with receiving reports from the classroom teacher and school specialists, it was meaningful to make personal observations of pupils in a classroom setting and to interact individually with them. In this way, I was able to observe directly the behaviors mentioned in the previous paragraph. This method for evaluating pupils was effective when the teacher and class were at ease with my presence. To facilitate such an open relationship, an effort was made to observe frequently and to develop rapport with pupils and classroom teachers both within and without the classroom. Whenever possible I participated in various activities with the pupils such as field trips, dances, assemblies, etc. This observation and interaction gave further insight into a pupil's personality, attitudes, and skills. It provided an opportunity to observe whether a pupil had intelligible speech, his level of receptive language ability, his attention span in a group as well as individually with me, and whether the pupil exhibited mannerisms that might be totally inappropriate in public. This type of relationship with classroom teachers and pupils was beneficial, for it provided firsthand data which was used to help identify pupils that might benefit from orientation and mobility instruction. It also proved helpful later as an assessment for entering behavior of those chosen as candidates.

After all the above data was collected, I had a clearer understanding of those pupils who were candidates for orientation and mobility instruction in use of public transportation facilities. Once the program was proven safe and feasible, a general rule was established. When doubt existed with regards to a particular pupil, he was given an opportunity.

## IDENTIFYING A CANDIDATE: A CASE STUDY

The following is a case study of the candidate identification process as discussed in the first part of this chapter. This is a study of Richard, an eighteen-year-old Down's syndrome pupil.

Richard was evaluated to determine if he would be a candidate for orientation and mobility instruction. In order to make a decision on his candidacy, I received input from Richard's current teacher, past teachers, record of his psychological testing results that included the psychologist's discussion and recommendations, and his workshop supervisor. In addition, my observation and interaction with Richard was an important consideration. The following written reports were helpful. They are in order: (1) psychologist's reports, discussion, and recommendations; (2) the Orientation and Mobility Information Form filled out by Richard's teacher; and (3) Richard's most recent report card.

*School Psychologists' Reports*

| 11/18/64 | Binet L-M | C.A. 7-10 | M.A. 2-11 | I.Q. 34 | |
|----------|-----------|-----------|-----------|---------|---|
| 12/19/67 | Binet L-M | C.A. 10-11 | M.A. 4-3 | I.Q. 42 | |
| 2/11/71 | Binet L-M | C.A. 14-1 | M.A. 5-4 | I.Q. 44 | |
| | Human Figure Drawing | | M.A. 6-3 | | |
| 10/15/74 | Binet L-M | C.A.17-9 | M.A. 5-6 | I.Q. 35 | |
| | Wide Range Achievement Tests | | Reading | Grade Equivalent 1.2 | |
| | | | Arithemtic | Grade Equivalent 1.2 | |
| | Draw-a-Man | | M.A. 6-3 | | |

11/18/64

Richard is a typical little mongoloid in appearance and

manner. He is friendly and happy and readily left his parents to come to the psychologist. In the examining room, he was cooperative and easily directed. He became involved in some of the items and wanted to repeat them. For example, in one item in which he had to find a cat hidden several times under one or another of several boxes, he insisted upon hiding it again for the psychologist to find.

Richard's mother said that she had been advised to place Richard in a state school but has not yet succeeded in doing so. She reported that he feeds himself and is toilet trained. He has evidently received love and good training at home. There is every reason to believe that he can adjust well in a training program. His mother was overjoyed to hear this and undoubtably will be cooperative.

### 12/19/67

Richard is pleasant and laughs readily. Presentation of problems sometimes struck him as funny, and he laughed hilariously. This laughter was shared with imaginary playmates. Earlier, he had drawn up a second chair, and his "playmate" sat in this chair. From time to time, he interacted with this playmate. Most of what Richard says sounds the same, and thus he cannot be scored higher than year III in vocabulary, though his comprehension is obviously beyond this point.

Richard responds well in class, though occasionally he becomes negativistic.

### 2/11/71

Richard is a large, obese, mongoloid youngster, who wears thick-lensed glasses. That Richard still has his imaginary playmate became known quickly. Looking over his right shoulder, he acknowledged his friend by waving and/or talking to him. Richard speaks in grunt fashion from the very back of his throat, which makes him extremely difficult to understand. To make matters worse, Richard habitually places his hand in front of his mouth when speaking. Additional help and effort at home and school are needed to alleviate this problem to a reasonable degree.

Educationally, Richard has the ability of a five and one-half-year-old. He can now print his name, count orally to seven, and reproduce geometrical designs characteristic of his mental age group. His teacher reported that Richard's social adjustment has improved significantly.

10/15/74

Richard did not allude to any imaginary playmates today; however, he did talk to himself a lot. He seemed pleased with his successes and he frequently pointed to his head in acknowledgement of his smartness. Richard cooperated fully in testing but preferred to point to things or describe them by outlining shapes with his fingers rather than try to say them. His speech, which is limited to single words, is difficult to understand; therefore, he would not handle any of the test items requiring expressive speech on the Binet.

On the Wide Range Achievement Test, Richard could read the letters of the alphabet. He counted 15 dots successfully, was able to read single-digit and some two-digit numbers. He printed his name very neatly.

## ORIENTATION AND MOBILITY INFORMATION SURVEY

Name __Richard_____ Age___18____

Address ____30001 Graham Blvd._____

Room No. _498_ IQ _35_ No. of Siblings ___3_____

Hearing Impairments_none_ Vision Impairments _20-50 with_
  _corrective lens_____

Speech Impairments __unintelligible_____

Other Physical Impairments __obese_____

Medical Impairments __none_____

1. Does pupil get along with his peers? __yes, but_____
   _generally keeps to self_____

2. Does pupil get along with familiar adults? __yes__

3. Does pupil get along with unfamiliar adults? __yes__

4. Does pupil deal appropriately with new and unexpected situations? __yes__

5. Does pupil exhibit any bizarre behaviorisms? __talks__ to himself

6. How long of a time period can pupil attend to a task in a group setting? __when he's interested, 45 minutes__

7. How long can the pupil attend to a task in a one-to-one situation? __45 minutes__

8. Does pupil follow directions? __yes, however there are__ times when he's stubborn

9. Can you rely on pupil to complete a task once it is begun? __yes__

10. Is pupil able to identify and distinguish green, yellow, and red? __yes__

11. Is pupil able to identify and distinguish green, yellow, and red signals of a traffic light? __yes__

12. Is pupil able to count objects? __yes, up to 15__

13. Can pupil recognize numerals? __one digit and some__ two-digit numbers

14. Is pupil able to identify money? __no__

15. Is pupil able to exchange money accurately? __no__

16. Can pupil read basic street signs? __yes__

17. Is pupil able to speak coherently? __no__

18. Is pupil able to communicate orally his or her home address and phone number? __no__

19. Is pupil able to use a public pay phone independently?

no
_____

20. Does pupil initiate conversation, or does he only respond once he is addressed?  he only responds in one-word answers

21. Does pupil initiate movement within classroom or building or does he wait for direction?  he generally waits for direction

22. Does pupil have to be told to do everything?  at times

Remarks  I don't think Richard will be able to use the public transit at this time

_____
_____
_____

------

*Report Card*
Conroy Center
Division for Exceptional Children
Pittsburgh Public Schools
Pittsburgh, Pennsylvania 15213

*Code:*
Y — Yes
P — Progressing
N — No
X — Does not apply

## ACADEMIC SKILLS

*Work Habits*
1. Follows directions ................................. P
2. Puts things away in proper place .................... Y
3. Works in a group .................................. P
4. Is accurate and completes tasks in given amount of
   time............................................. P

5. Takes pride in his work ............................. P
6. Accepts the fact that he makes mistakes .............. P
7. Works independently, organizes work, works
   consistently ........................................ P
8. Uses reason and common sense in problem solving .... P

*Number Work*

1. Recognizes numbers (1-10, 1-20, 1-50, 1-100) .......... P
2. Counts objects (1-10, 1-15, 1-20, 1-50, 1-100) .......... Y
3. Reads and uses telephone dial ........................ N
4. Tells time on hour, 1/2 hour, 1/4 hour .............. P
5. Recognizes coins..................................... P
6. Counts money (1-5¢, 1-10¢, 1-25¢, 50¢, $1.00, over
   $1.00) ............................................. N
7. Measures with a ruler, yardstick ..................... N
8. Recognizes pint, quart, 1/2 gallon ................... P

*Conceptual Skills*

1. Recognizes names in print: self, others .............. P
2. Recognizes similarities and differences: color,
   size, shape, number ............................... P
3. Reads color words, number words .................... N
4. Reads and matches according to color, size, no., etc. ... P
5. Reads words needed for everyday living .............. N
6. Arranges numbers in a series ........................ P
7. Differentiates between opposites...................... P
8. Reads timetables and schedules, newspapers, simple
   books, for pleasure ................................ N

*Sensory Skills*

1. Differentiates between same and different sounds ....... Y
2. Identifies and categories sounds...................... P
3. Distinguishes between pleasant and unpleasant
   smells, tastes ..................................... Y
4. Matches objects that feel the same or different
   without looking.................................... P

*Motor Skills*

*Gross — Large Muscle*

1. Moves easily from one place to another with, without
   aid, (floor, chair, cab) ........................... Y
2. Moves about in coordinated manner on smooth
   surfaces........................................... Y

3. Moves about in coordinated manner on variable surfaces
   (stairs, curbs, ramps, outdoor surfaces) .............. Y

*Fine — Small Muscle*
1. Uses hands in reaching, grasping, holding ........... Y
2. Uses eye-hand coordination in pincer and grasp
   movements ........................................ Y
3. Uses pencil, brush, crayons, scissors, paste properly .... Y
4. Uses complex puzzles and building toys .............. N
5. Manipulates locks, latches, lids, switches, zippers ...... Y
6. Pours without spilling ............................. Y

## LANGUAGE SKILLS

*Receptive*
1. Pays attention when spoken to ...................... Y
2. Replies to questions adequately ..................... P
3. Listens to and carries out directions ................ Y
4. Listens in group situations ......................... P
5. Understands a story ................................ P
6. Can answer phone .................................. P

*Expressive*
1. Recognizes and indicates need for help .............. Y
2. Speaks clearly ..................................... N
3. Speaks in whole sentences .......................... N
4. Refers to self as I ................................. P
5. Carries on meaningful conversation with peers, adults .. P
6. Relates facts about self and environment: name,
   address, phone, parent's name ..................... P
7. Asks questions .................................... P
8. Knows how to use the telephone adequately ........... N

*Prevocational Skills*
1. Is able to do the following with some proficiency
   a. Cut ............................................ Y
   b. Sort ........................................... Y
   c. Stack .......................................... Y
   d. Count .......................................... P
   e. Fold ........................................... Y
   f. Stuff .......................................... Y
   g. Staple ......................................... Y

    h. Clip ............................................. Y
    i. Other ...........................................

*Mobility*

1. Gets into and out of cab unaided.................... Y
2. Crosses streets alone ............................... N
3. Can use public transportation independently ......... N
4. Travels independently within school building ........ Y

## SOCIAL SKILLS

*Awareness of Others*

1. Works with others ................................... Y
2. Accepts and gives help.............................. Y
3. Seeks attention of others .......................... Y
4. Respects rights of others .......................... Y
5. Shares ............................................. Y
6. Shows concern and affection for others............... Y
7. Participates in leisure-time activities with others ....... Y
8. Plays group games and follows rules................. Y
9. Chooses activities appropriate for his age............. Y

*Emotional*

1. Behaves within defined limits ....................... Y
2. Controls temper .................................... P
3. Accepts criticism................................... Y
4. Reacts appropriately to social situation............... Y
5. Has a sense of humor ............................... Y
6. Shows respect for peers, authority................... Y

## SELF-CARE SKILLS

*Body Awareness*

1. Touches and names body parts ...................... P
2. Recognizes self, others as male or female ............. Y
3. Accepts changes in body as he matures............... Y

*Eating Habits*

1. Opens own lunch and milk .......................... Y
2. Knows proper utensils to use with various types of
    foods ............................................. Y
3. Uses napkin properly ............................... Y
4. Uses eating utensils properly ....................... Y

5. Opens, pours, drinks from straw, glass ................. Y
6. Indicates likes and dislikes for certain foods ........... Y
7. Tries new foods ...................................... P
8. Has good table manners ............................. Y
9. Cleans up after himself ............................. Y

*Dressing Skills*

1. Puts on or removes coat, etc., with, without aid ....... Y
2. Chooses clothing appropriate for weather, age, sex ..... Y
3. Hangs coat on hook, hanger ......................... Y
4. Cares for clothing and personal belongings............ Y
5. Recognizes need for laundering and repair of
   clothing ............................................. Y

*Personal Hygiene*

1. Recognizes need for clean body parts.................. Y
2. Identifies and properly uses items of oral, nasal
   hygiene............................................. Y
3. Combs own hair ................................... Y
4. Cares for nails, shaving, feminine hygiene............. P
5. Takes pride in his appearance ....................... Y
6. Performs toileting procedure with, without aid ........ Y
7. Cares for own items of feminine or masculine
   hygiene............................................. Y

## A SKETCH OF RICHARD

Using the above written information in conjunction with discussion with key staff members and my personal observations, I developed the following sketch of Richard. The outline is based on the four basic requisites discussed earlier that provided the criteria for consideration of orientation and mobility candidacy.

### Social Emotional Adjustment

Richard demonstrates appropriate social skills by participating adequately when a member of a group such as in the classroom or workshop setting. According to input from his teacher and workshop supervisor Richard works well with others, accepts and gives help, seeks attention of others, respects rights of others, shares, shows concern for others, participates in leisure-time activities with others, plays group games and follows rules, and chooses activities appropriate for his age. Richard's speech is unintelligible, but his speech is assisted somewhat by effective skills in pantomime. In this way, Richard is able in a limited manner to communicate his needs and feelings to peers and adults. In my observation of Richard in the community while on field trips, he appeared to be well adjusted and behaved in an appropriate manner.

In regards to his emotional adjustment, Richard behaves in the classroom and workshop within defined limits, accepts criticism, reacts appropriately to social situations, has a sense of humor, and shows respect for peers and staff members. At infrequent times, Richard demonstrates difficulty controlling his temper, although the staff reports that Richard is maturing with age in this respect. When Richard is upset and is unable to communicate his problem, he displays what is described as stubborn behavior. There are times when Richard demonstrates what might be considered abnormal behavior; he talks to himself. While this may not be considered normal, this behavior does not occur frequently and should not inhibit his success on the public transit. Generally Richard's demonstrated social and emotional adjustment appears to be adequate for consideration as a candidate for orientation and mobility instruction.

### *Learning Basic Routines*

Although Richard has limited communication skills, his receptive language ability is good; he understands directions. His teacher and workshop supervisor report that while not competent at this point, Richard is making progress in the following work habits: learning to follow directions, working in a group, being accurate and completing tasks in a given amount of time, taking pride in his work, accepting the fact that he makes mistakes, working independently, and using common sense in problem solving. His attention span in the classroom and work tolerance in the workshop are adequate. At infrequent periods when Richard is upset, his stubborn behavior affects his work. Another problem is that, at times, his speaking to himself may interfere with his work performance. However, he generally learns classroom and workshop routines and is able to perform them satisfactorily.

## Numeral Discrimination

Richard is able to recognize one digit and some two-digit numbers. One concern was raised about his visual acuity of 20/50 with correction. His teacher made up numeral flash cards. Richard was asked to identify these numerals from a distance to simulate the situation he would encounter in the community. He was able to succeed in this simulation, but more valid data would be obtained once he is in the real situation.

## Making Action Decisions and Initiating Movement

This might be an area of potential problems. While Richard is well behaved, he does seem to require direction and supervision. And yet, the center is organized in such a way that it is difficult to assess whether a pupil can initiate his own behavior. As is true in group settings, the pupils at the center are rewarded more for acquiescent behavior than for the self-initiation of behavior. However, on occasions, Richard demonstrates a limited sense of independence. He carries out assignments such as delivering items to the center office and other points within the building without direction. It appears that Richard can learn to initiate movement that is required for orientation and mobility instruction.

# Chapter 4

# ATTAINING PARENTAL COOPERATION— AND COMMITMENT————————————————

If you can teach my daughter to ride the public bus to the center, I'll eat my hat!

A Parent

**A**FTER I identified pupils as candidates for orientation and mobility instruction, my next step was to seek the permission of their parents. This was a critical phase, for without parental permission as well as support and commitment, there is no orientation and mobility program.

Parents were hesitant to allow their retarded children to travel independently. They felt this way because they were not aware that mentally retarded persons were capable of traveling independently; they were fearful for their children's safety while traveling in the community, and they were quite content with the traditional system of cab transportation provided for their child. For these reasons, it was understandable that parents were hesitant.

They had not been informed that a specialized instructional program could teach mentally retarded persons to learn independent travel skills. Prior to the initiation of our program, most parents as well as professionals just assumed that independent travel was beyond the realm of the mentally retarded person's capability. The success of past programs had not reached the attention of others.

Parental fears for the safety of their child were not totally unrealistic. Cortazzo and Sansone (1969), in establishing their travel training program for adult retarded persons, listed many of the common anxieties expressed by parents:

   1. Sexual molestation

2. Kidnapping
3. Injuries or accidents
4. Getting lost
5. Ridicule by others
6. Failure to learn because of retardation
7. Helplessness in emergencies
8. Physical stress on the health of the retarded
9. Dangers in traveling in inclement weather
10. Failure to recognize impending dangers or hazardous situations
11. Detriment to parents' already precarious health because of worry [p. 68].

Parents were faced with daily horror stories sensationally presented in the daily newspaper and television news.

Furthermore, parents were accustomed to having transportation provided for their children; they accepted this as natural and necessary. They felt satisfied that their children were traveling every day to school, and there was no apparent reason for thinking differently or changing from this tradition.

Consequently, the suggestion that their child was being considered as a candidate for orientation and mobility instruction often caused a great deal of anxiety. My task was to intervene at that stage of their frustration.

## PARENT INTERVENTION STRATEGY

The parent intervention strategy I chose had its theoretical basis in a book by Chris Argyris (1970). Although Argyris' work is concerned with intervention as it related to organizational change, his theory also seemed applicable to my intervention with parents. Argyris (1970) defined an intervention as a process where one:

is to enter into an ongoing system of relationship, to come between or among persons, groups, or objects for the purpose of helping them [p. 15].

I was the intervenor who must enter into an ongoing system of relationships, the family, for the purpose of helping them to provide for the adjustment of their mentally retarded child. Argyris stated that there are three processes that he called primary tasks of any intervention activity. They include (1) valid and useful information, (2) free choice, and (3) internal commitment (1970). I will elucidate how these primary tasks were used as the basis for my dealing with parents.

### Valid Information

Valid information, according to Argyris, is "that which describes the factors, plus their interrelationship, that create the problem for the client system" (1970, p. 17). As an intervenor, I provided parents with valid and useful information in order to help them make a judgment.

The parents had lacked the required information that many mentally retarded persons are capable of traveling independently. I cited as evidence persons within our present program who had been successful in using public transportation facilities. Since parents of retarded pupils tend to be a closely knit group, some had already been aware of a friend's child who had learned independent travel skills. It was helpful at times to refer one parent to other parents whose child had participated in orientation and mobility instruction. Communicating with other parents was quite informative and comforting to the parent of a prospective candidate.

Besides informing parents that mentally retarded persons can travel independently as the result of specialized instruction, I informed the parents that the instruction is a safe process. The parents learned that there would be a one-to-one instructor-pupil ratio and that my first priority was the safety of their child. I informed parents that the instructor would work with a pupil for as long a time as is needed to learn the skills. There are no time constraints. Only after the pupil had demonstrated competence would he be permitted to travel alone.

The parents and I discussed what independent travel could mean to the pupil. They came to realize that the sense of performing an adult function, having to depend on oneself, and having the ability to travel independently to a future job placement are important to a retarded citizen.

After viewing the value of independent travel to the pupil, we discussed what the pupil's travel independence could mean to them: it would reduce the dependence on them to drive their young adult to work daily, or to take him shopping or to some leisure-time activity. A great deal of time as well as money could be saved by having a pupil initiate his own travel. Parents were surprised to learn that their child would have an opportunity to acquire travel skills but were relieved to know that such competence would permit him to function more independently as an adult in the future.

## Free Choice

Once accurate information was provided and questions answered, I explained to the parents that it was totally their decision whether or not their child would participate in the orientation and mobility instruction program. This is the second primary task, free choice. According to Argyris, free choice "places the locus of decision making in the client system [family]" (1970, p. 19). The parents must have the autonomy to decide whether their child shall or shall not receive orientation and mobility instruction. After considering what they had learned about the instruction process, its possible effect on them, and its possible effect on their child, they made the final decision. For without free choice there was little chance for commitment and support during the subsequent instructional process.

## Internal Commitment

This led to the third primary task, internal commitment. Argyris defined internal commitment as:

> ... the course of action or choice that has been internalized by the [parents] ... so that they experience a high degree of ownership and have a feeling of responsibility about the choice and its implications [p. 20].

If the parents gave their consent, they were then committed to their action by their own forces and not induced forces; they then became involved in the process and shared in its success. They were involved in the planning process and the implementation of the instruction.

After the parents gave permission for their child to participate in orientation and mobility instruction, the travel route was planned with their help. Many parents had a knowledge of public bus routes and were helpful in choosing the most appropriate ones for their child. It was necessary in many cases to choose a route that was longer but safer over one that was more direct and less safe. If parents were unsure of the bus route, I consulted with the transit authority for detailed information.

Once a successful program had been established and a number of persons had learned independent travel skills, I initiated a thorough public relations campaign. At parents' meetings, I informed the parent group of the success of those pupils who had learned independent travel; I presented pupils with a certificate of merit at such meetings. Articles for the school newsletter and the local daily newspaper were written describing the orientation and mobility program and the success of individuals who benefited from the program. I contacted local television stations, and they made a report on the program. Through this strategy, I was successful in communicating the message of the success to many other parents. The possibility that their child could succeed helped raise their expectations for their child; it also reduced their anxiety.

## CONSULTING WITH MARK'S PARENTS

Mark had been identified as a candidate for orientation and mobility instruction. The following is a case study that depicts the process of seeking permission and support from Mark's parents. It is based on the typical experience that the orientation and mobility instructor may encounter in dealing with parents in such an anxiety evoking situation.

Since enrolling in the public schools, Mark had been transported daily to and from the center by taxi. The taxi driver would pull up to the front of Mark's house in the morning, and in the afternoon, the taxi driver would release Mark to his waiting parents. This was a safe, convenient, and reliable means of transportation, and Mark's parents were quite content with this system. Although Mark's parents had learned that a friend's daughter had learned to travel independently to the center via public transit, they felt that this was only because she had more ability than Mark. They felt that Mark was not capable of using the public transit and avoided any thought of Mark's possible travel independence. It was acceptable for another's son or daughter but not for their son.

I called Mark's parents and made an appointment to talk with them in their home. Mark's parents listened closely as I described both my role as orientation and mobility instructor and the number of pupils that had learned independent travel skills as the result of the orientation and mobility program. I suggested that as a result of my evaluation made in conjunction with Mark's classroom teacher, workshop supervisor, and other staff members, I thought Mark would make a good candidate for orientation and mobility instruction. Mark's parents responded by saying that they were quite fearful of their son's traveling alone on the public transit.

I explained to them that the manner in which the orientation and mobility program was designed made it a safe process; I would work on a one-to-one basis with Mark. Mark and I would meet at the center and his daily lessons would consist of us taking the public bus from the center to his home and then making the return trip. Initially, I would stay close to Mark and give him direction and support. Gradually, I would move away from him and permit him to initiate movement through the route. In later lessons, I would simply follow Mark's lead to evaluate his competence. Only after Mark demonstrated to me that he was able to negotiate the travel route safely and independently would I permit him to travel alone; there would be no time constraints. Mark and I would practice the trip for as long a time period as Mark might require to learn the trip.

I then mentioned what travel independence would mean to Mark and to them, his parents. Mark would be performing an adult function. He would learn to depend on his own decisions and would develop a greater positive concept of his own worth and independence. It was also mentioned that Mark's travel independence would relieve possible anxieties they might have over his future. After public school, Mark would have the skills and confidence to travel independently to his future vocational placement site. It would reduce his dependence on his parents for transportation to work, shopping, and leisure-time activities. Mark's parents responded saying that indeed they had been anxious about how Mark would be able to function once they were gone from his life.

I explained that having Mark ride the public transit to the center would not result in any expense to the family. The Board of Education provided the bus passes.

During my explanations and after these points were made, I responded to their questions, and we discussed their fears. I explained that their fears were realistic and were shared by other parents whose sons or daughters entered orientation and mobility instruction. Again it was reaffirmed that Mark was capable of being a successful traveler, and they were encouraged to give their permission. It was clear that they did have a choice. My feeling was expressed that I hoped they would give Mark an opportunity to demonstrate to us that he was capable. Mark's parents said that they would talk it over, and I agreed to call them the next day to discuss this further.

The next day I called, and Mark's parents agreed to permit him to receive orientation and mobility instruction and for him to travel independently to the center upon successful completion of instruction. They provided some information that clarified which would be the best bus for Mark to use to travel to the downtown district. I explained that during the instructional process I would call them frequently to report on Mark's progress.

After two weeks of daily orientation and mobility instruction, Mark demonstrated competence to travel to and from the center independently; he became a safe and independent traveler. A few months later, Mark's parents were interviewed for the purpose of discussing their reaction to my intervention and Mark's success as an independent traveler. Mark's parents were willing to discuss freely in retrospect their feelings during this process. The following are excerpts from that interview:

Q: *What was your first reaction when I suggested that Mark begin orientation and mobility instruction?*

A: (Mark's Father) I was afraid to let him on his own. I was afraid to make him go back and forth to town or wherever he had to go. It was something I didn't think I had the guts to let him do. I didn't think he would be able to do it. In fact, even before this, I would not permit him to do much alone, and I did most things for him. I never dreamed that Mark could travel to the center or go to town or travel on any public vehicle by himself. I didn't think he could do it, and I was afraid to allow him to do it.

Q: *What were some of your concerns about Mark eventually traveling independently to the center?*

A: (Mark's Father) I think the first thing that hit me was that if he were to travel by himself, he might not be alert enough to cross streets safely. He might not look both ways and not know when a car had his turn signal on to turn right. My first fear was that he just wouldn't be safe. The second fear was perhaps he would get on the wrong bus, and he would get lost. I just couldn't see him recognizing the bus numerals, getting on the bus, using correct change, getting off, walking several blocks, getting on another bus, and getting to his appointed destination; and the same thing on the return trip.

(Mark's Mother) Frankly, I was worried about someone taking advantage of him. I didn't know whether he was capable. To be honest, we weren't the type to really let him go out on his own much.

Q: *What made you decide to permit Mark to participate in orientation and mobility instruction?*

A: (Mark's Father) My wife had more confidence than I did. I almost said no because I was afraid for him. I just worried. But I realized that one day he would have to do it by himself when neither myself, his mother, or his brothers were here to shelter him the way that I have tried to do. And I finally realized that. After meeting you, it gave me the confidence that I should have had in the beginning. That's what made me go along with it. But there was a doubt

whether I should go along with it because of my fears ...
When we had our conference with you I was impressed with
your manner. I can usually tell when someone has the patience. It's difficult for a person who has not lived with a
retarded person to have feelings and patience for a young
man like Mark. As a father I didn't think anyone could feel
what you feel. After my wife and I decided to go ahead and
try this, I felt comfortable. Him in your hands was all right
with me.

(Mark's Mother) When you came to our house, I could see the
warmth about you. You made us feel confident. After our
discussion, I thought that Mark had to learn sometime.
When you insisted that he would be safe, we felt we would
take the chance. I am grateful for that. When you visited us,
it was your attitude that impressed us. A lot of people in the
field of mental retardation are cold. I don't think they mean
to be that way, but I think they feel that they know what
they are talking about, and they just go on and say, "Well,
you should do this, and you should do that." You didn't act
that way. You came in and made us feel like Mark belonged
to you as well as us. You gave us a choice. You made us feel
that what you were telling us was true or you wouldn't have
been sitting there telling us it. This is what made me feel
that you were capable of teaching my son to travel. You
were warm and understanding. You explained to us that
you understood the situation and you said that most people
do have this fear. You said that once you let Mark go, he
would be capable of more things than we thought. And I
found this to be true. You didn't come in and say, "Well,
I'm going to teach Mark mobility." You didn't do this. You
gave us a choice. That's what made me feel more secure ...

Chapter 5

# THE MAKING OF AN INDEPENDENT _____
# TRAVELER: THE THEORY _____

> A true learning situation is a problem-solving situation. It is common in life outside on an individual basis ... The only place in life where we do not follow the typical learning procedures, oddly enough, is in school, where people are presumably assembled for the express purpose of learning.
>
> Earl C. Kelly
> *The Workshop Way of Learning*

THIS chapter presents a theoretical framework that is the basis for the teaching of independent travel skills. The focus for instruction is the teaching of skills to enable pupils to use public transit facilities independently on one basic route: between home and the center. While the reader might be tempted to believe that skills in basic sidewalk travel, crossing streets, and business district travel ought to be taught prior to use of the public transit, this is not the case. These skills, which might seem to be prerequisite ones, cannot be learned with retention unless there is a purpose and an opportunity to use these skills daily. The instruction of a method of travel and the subsequent independent travel via the public transit in lieu of taxicabs or vans provide this purpose and opportunity to utilize and retain learned travel skills.

My teaching strategy was based on five steps for the instruction of skills outlined by John P. De Cecco (1968). The steps are: (1) "Analyzing the Skill," (2) "Assessing the Entering Behavior of the Student," (3) "Arranging for Training in the Component Units," (4) "Describing and Demonstrating the Skill," and (5) "Providing for the Three Basic Learning Conditions" [pp. 306-318]. These five steps for teaching skills provide the structure for this chapter.

## ANALYZING THE SKILL

Since skilled performance involves a chain of motor responses, and this organization of stimulus response chains (S-R) makes up larger response patterns, my first step was to analyze the skills involved in independent use of the public bus in terms of S-R units (De Cecco, 1968). Together they make up the larger response pattern of independent public bus travel. The S-R units involved in riding the public bus from the center to home are the following:

S Identify bus-stop sign
↓
R Stand by the bus-stop sign

•

S Identify bus
↓
R Enter bus

•

S Face driver
↓
R Pay fare

•

S Identify unoccupied seat
↓
R Sit down

•

S Identify landmarks for alighting
↓
R Ring buzzer

•

S Door opens
↓
R Alight from bus

•

S Faced with familiar neighborhood
↓
R Walk home

The skills in this sequence satisfy what Thomas F. Gilbert

terms "a chain of behaviors" (1962). In "Mathetics: The Technology of Education," Gilbert defines the concept of chain of behaviors (1962):

(a) *Chain.* Behavior can be thought of as a sequence of events having three properties: a *response*, some occasion for that response (called a stimulus), and some consequence that makes the response more or less likely. to occur again on the same occasion. If the effect produced by the response makes it *more* likely to occur again, that effect is called a *reinforcer.* A behavior chain is a sequence of stimuli, responses, and reinforcers in which the reinforcer for one response is also the stimulus for the next response. We symbolically represent a chain in this way:

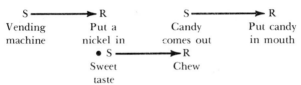

In this example the first stimulus (S) sets the occasion for the first response; the response is reinforced by the appearance of candy which becomes the stimulus for the second response. The reinforcer of the second response is the stimulus for the third response. The unity of the behavior chain is determined by this reciprocal relation in which responses produce stimuli and stimuli alone has any behavioral meaning unless viewed in relation to each other [p. 217].

According to Gilbert, the first requirement of a chain of behaviors is that the final outcome be a reinforcer (1962). The final outcome of the bus trip, locating home, is a strong reinforcer to a pupil. While the pupil travels via public bus, most of the travel route is initially unfamiliar; this is true until the pupil alights from the bus in his neighborhood. When he sights his neighborhood, the pupil's uncertainty of an unfamiliar trip changes to feelings of confidence in an area where he is more at ease. The arrival to a familiar home environment with knowledge of completion of a successful trip provides a strong reinforcement to the pupil.

The second requirement, according to Gilbert, for a process to be a chain of behaviors is that the individual behaviors be linked through the formula, S→R • S→R (1962). The above analysis of the component skills of using a public bus indicates that there is such a relationship. In the sequence, each stimulus requires and sets the occasion for the response. There is, as Gilbert states, a reciprocal relation in which responses produce stimuli and stimuli produce responses. There is no behavioral meaning of each stimulus and response unless viewed in relation to one another (Gilbert, 1962).

As a result of the above analysis, independent travel was viewed as a chain of behaviors composed of (S-R) units. With a clear analysis of the (S-R) units and their interrelationship in component units, my next consideration was to assess the entering behavior of the pupils.

## ASSESSING THE ENTERING BEHAVIOR

The second step in the teaching process was the assessment of entering behavior. De Cecco (1968) defined entering behavior as:

> the behavior the student must have acquired before he can acquire particular new terminal behaviors. More simply, entering behavior describes the present status of the student's knowledge and skill in reference to a future status the teacher wants him to attain [p. 59].

With knowledge of a pupil's entering behavior, those skills which the pupil had prior to instruction, I was able to more appropriately plan lessons with a focus on those specific component skills that required intensive instruction. The assessment of entering behavior came from three sources: (1) the candidate identification process, (2) a parent interview, and (3) lessons with the pupil on the public transit.

As described earlier in the candidate identification process, four basic requisite skills provided the criteria for selection of those pupils who might benefit from orientation and mobility instruction in the use of public transportation facilities. In addition, this process provided information concerning an individual pupil's entering behavior. The assessment of these skills were helpful in the planning for individualized lessons.

The second source in the assessment of entering behavior was a parent interview. During the candidate identification process, parents are not consulted to gain information on pupils because the timing was premature; I wanted to be certain that a particular pupil was capable of success before the family was contacted. However, once the parent intervention was made and the parents gave permission for their young adult to participate in the orientation and mobility program, they provided further data for a more complete assessment of entering behavior.

The parents were interviewed in their home setting; they provided information regarding the pupil's experience using the public transit. Through this interview, it was learned if the pupil was permitted to play independently in the neighborhood, how far the pupil was permitted to play away from home, if the pupil made independent purchases at neighborhood businesses, if the family normally used the public transit, and if the pupil had had past experiences using the public transit. The following questionnaire is an outline of questions whose answers helped assess entering behavior in order that lessons could more appropriately be planned.

## PARENT INTERVIEW FORM

Name _____

Parent of _____

Address _____

1. Does you child play unsupervised in your neighborhood?

   _____

2. How far is your child permitted to play away from home?

   _____

3. Does your child travel independently to a friend or relative's home? _____

4. Does your child travel independently and make purchases at a local business? _____

   _____

5. Is your child able to handle money responsibly? _____

   _____

6. Does your family routinely use public transportation? ____

   _____

7. Has your child used a public transit bus in your company?

_____

   How often? _____
8. Where has your child traveled by public transit while accompanied by others? _____
   How often? _____
9. Does your child regularly use a public bus? _____

_____

   For what purpose? _____

_____

Comments _____

_____

_____

_____

_____

_____

_____

_____

_____

Basically, the answers to these questions described the extent to which the pupil was permitted to move about his environment, and whether or not the movement was independent or with the supervision of an adult or sibling. The response to the interview ranged between two extremes; the pupil had total freedom, or he was permitted little freedom of movement, even within his neighborhood. In the first case, the pupil was termed a "street kid," for he spent many hours per day away from home; he had varied experiences using public transit with friends, siblings, or alone. In such cases, his parents generally relied on public transit for transportation, and thus he often accompanied his parents on shopping trips, etc. In the other extreme, the pupil was totally protected by his family and was not even permitted outside to play. Obviously this latter group's entering behavior lacked many skills and experiences possessed by the former group.

While the candidate identification process and the parent

interview provided data as to the entering behavior of a pupil, perhaps the most significant information became apparent during the lessons using the public transit. By careful observation, I was able to evaluate what skills the pupil brought into the instruction process and those that will require intensive work.

## ARRANGING FOR TRAINING IN THE COMPONENT UNITS

After collecting and analyzing the entering behavior data, in most cases the pupils needed instruction in some of the component skills. This is the third step in the skill-teaching process. According to De Cecco (1968), training in the component units:

> provides the student with the opportunity to learn missing S-R links or component skills ... and provides the student with the opportunity to learn the skill components (or some of them) so well that he can focus his attention on the new aspects of the complex task he is learning [p. 309].

The training in component units was facilitated either by myself, the classroom teacher, parents, or a combination of the above. The following were component units that generally required additional work: paying the fare, identification of bus numerals, and identification of landmarks for alighting from the bus.

Some pupils required practice in learning to pay their fare. They needed may repetitions to learn the following sequence: take their wallet out of their pocket or purse, open the wallet, display their bus pass to the driver, deposit a ten-cent ticket in the fare box, indicate to the driver that they wish a transfer receipt, hold the transfer receipt in one hand, close the wallet, and return the wallet to their pocket. This sequence was practiced through repetitious simulation activities as well as verbal review.

The component unit of numeral recognition was learned through a variety of instructional activities. One activity was to use flash cards; these cards contained numerals of all the buses that stopped at the pupil's bus stop. From this set of numerals, the pupil was required to identify his correct bus numeral. A derivation of this activity was quite successful, but it required photographic assistance. With the help of our media specialist, a set of slides were prepared that consisted of the front view pictures of all the public buses that stopped at the pupil's transit stop. Again, the pupil was required to identify "his" bus from the larger set of buses pictured by the slide presentation. Also, an effective activity was to have the pupil circle the "correct" bus numeral on a worksheet that listed a large set of numerals.

The identification of landmarks for alighting from the bus was another component unit that required special instruction. Practicing the identification of landmarks generally was facilitated by verbal review. Another activity was to have the pupil draw pictures of the specific landmark along his route. For example, if the landmark for a pupil to alight from the bus was a pizza shop and a gas station, the pupil would draw pictures of those landmarks. These pictures then were used to verbally review the route. One parent had her daughter draw a pizza shop, the landmark for her to alight from the bus, and she taped it on the refrigerator door at home as a constant reminder to her daughter.

These are just some activities that were used, and they are suggestions of many activities that may be developed by the enterprising orientation and mobility instructor, classroom teacher, or parent.

## DESCRIBING AND DEMONSTRATING THE SKILL

This step involved the actual instruction of the pupil on an individualized route between school and home. Unlike Kubat (1973), who used an agency van to act as a mock bus for simulation purposes prior to the instruction on the public bus, I used regularly scheduled public buses to teach the route. This decision was based on the tenet that mentally retarded persons learn more efficaciously "by doing" rather than simulating a task and then having to transfer their learning to a real setting. While simulation activities do play an important role in learning component skills, my position was that a real experience should be provided for the pupil, and this meant using the public bus from the very beginning.

During the instructional process, the pupil continued to travel to the center by his normal means (taxi or van), and I met him at the center. From the center as the starting point, we made the complete trip to his home and back to the center. Only one basic route was taught; there was no instruction to any objective other than the basic trip. The rationale was that the pupil had to learn the skills and become comfortable with one basic route before he could be expected to travel to different destinations or use alternate routes.

This step required directive instruction. The pupil was given a bus pass for his wallet and would pay the fare after I demonstrated what was involved in this task. I stayed physically close to the pupil and explained what to do, what not to do, and how to behave while proceeding through each component unit.

In this phase, particularly, I was conscious of my own behavior, for I was a model that the pupil emulated. Although verbal instructions were meaningful, significant learning occurred through the model of my behavior; in every sense, I attempted to model the "consummate bus rider." When I took a seat that was empty, I moved to one side of the seat so as to leave room for another person; I attended to where the bus was moving by looking out the window; if a conversation started with another passenger, it was short, and care was taken to attend to the window in order to demonstrate behavior that results in orientation maintenance.

Throughout this step, the process was one simply of demonstration of the component units. In many cases, the pupil was quite bewildered by such a change in his daily routine. I proceeded with verbal instruction carefully depending on a particular pupil's readiness. No feedback was given to the pupil; little was demanded at this point.

## PROVIDING FOR THE BASIC LEARNING CONDITIONS

In the skill-learning process, according to De Cecco, there are three basic learning conditions: contiguity, practice, and feedback (1968). De Cecco (1968) stated that:

> ... we must usually provide them concurrently rather than
> sequentially. More simply, much of your success in teaching
> a skill will depend not only on how well you provide for each
> of these learning conditions but also on how skillfully you
> can combine them into a single teaching situation [p. 313].

In this step, I will define each of these three basic learning
conditions and demonstrate how they were used in the teaching
process.

### Contiguity

Contiguity as defined by De Cecco (1968), is the condition
that provides for "the almost simultaneous occurrence of the
stimulus and the response" [p. 284]. He further stated that:

> To meet this condition you must teach the student proper
> coordination and timing. For proper coordination the student
> must learn the proper order, or sequence, of the units of
> subtasks of the skill. For proper timing, the adjacent units in
> a chain or adjacent subtasks in a hierarchy must occur simul-
> taneously, without delay and unnecessary pauses [p. 313].

In one published training program, the contiguity was provided by breaking the travel route into subtasks which were
termed "manageable units" (Cortazzo & Sansone, 1969). In this
design, the authors stated:

> Instructors selected the outstanding cues along the route. The
> trainee went through the complete route several times with
> the instructor. Following this the route was broken down into
> what were considered manageable units. What constituted a
> manageable unit depended on the trainee's ability and the
> complexity of the route. The staff estimated that a manage-
> able unit should take a trainee no longer than a maximum of
> two weeks to learn. Each unit had to be mastered before the
> next one in route sequence was attempted. Each unit learned
> was traveled every day so that there was a tendency to over-
> learn the units. When the trainee mastered all the route units,
> the instructor would let him lead the way for the complete
> route [p. 75].

Cortazzo and Sansone were successful in teaching the subtasks in the sequence that they occurred in the travel route; they did not introduce the next subtask until the previous subtasks had been mastered. Contiguity of instruction was provided by teaching the second subtask while practicing the mastered first subtask. Once the second subtask was mastered, they proceeded to the third subtask while still practicing the first and second subtasks. This continued until all the subtasks were learned (and overlearned) in order, and thus the complete route was learned.

However, use of the manageable unit approach raises some questions. Was the use of the instruction time less than efficient in that the pupil lacked an overall perspective of the total trip? The pupil did not experience an overview of a completed trip with the extrinsic reward of reaching one's destination until the final stages of the instruction process. Another question deals with the logistics of the instruction. What was the procedure when the instruction of a subtask brought the pupil halfway into the route? The authors stated that the next subtask was not introduced until the previous one was mastered. Does this mean that the lesson was terminated midway in the route? Did they conclude the lesson and find some way to return to the center which might result in confusion for the pupil?

Unlike the program of Cortazzo and Sansone, my program provided for contiguity by using a backward chaining sequence for instruction of each component unit while taking the pupil through the complete route each lesson. This reverse contiguity was used since the task of learning to independently use a public bus involved a sequence defined by Gilbert as a chain of behaviors (1962). According to Gilbert, the most efficient method for the teaching of a chain of behaviors is to first teach the final behaviors in the chain. The reason, he asserts, is that the final behavior is always learned first, regardless of the order behaviors are presented in instruction (1962).

In teaching the chain of behaviors in using a public bus, I demonstrated the respective skill sequence in the order that it is normally practiced. This sequence is outlined in the first step, analyzing the skill. However, the final component was the focus for instruction; this was the component where the pupil located home. Although the pupil and I experienced the complete trip, the instruction began with the final component in the chain and proceeded in a backwards sequence. After the final skill was mastered, the next component in the chain became the focus etc. According to Robert C. Hogan (1975):

> Teaching the operants in a backward sequence might be a more efficient method of teaching those chains because the reinforcer is attained immediately after the last operant is completed, and the stimulus which is the occasion for the response becomes a conditioned reinforcer so that the next operant might be more efficiently learned also [p. 29].

After a number of bus trip repetitions, the pupil learned the complete sequence and was able to independently use the bus for the specific route. This theory was used as the basis for this training program.

## Practice

According to De Cecco (1968), the second basic learning condition is practice, which he defines as "the repetition of a response in the presence of the stimulus" [p. 249]. The tired old cliché of "practice makes perfect" is quite applicable. Repetition was a key condition for teaching independent travel on the public bus. Once we began practicing the bus route, we worked every day until the pupil was able to perform the complete task independently; we spent as many repetitions as necessary for a pupil to learn the trip. Each round-trip lesson took a half day, so two pupils per day received instruction; I made every effort not to miss a day's practice. Depending on the level of a pupil's entering behavior, it took between four days and four weeks of daily instruction with the average time being two and one-half weeks per pupil.

## Feedback

Feedback, the third basic learning condition, is defined by De Cecco (1968) as "the information available to the student which makes possible the comparison of his actual performance with some standard performance of a skill" [p. 290]. In teaching independent travel skills, verbal feedback acted as the reinforcer. The pupil's knowledge that he was performing a task correctly was rewarding, and the pupil tended to repeat rewarded responses. By selectively reinforcing appropriate behaviors, it was possible to shape the behavior of the pupils so they were able to respond appropriately in each unit of the component chain. This process is discussed by Winfred F. Hill (1963):

> ... behavior ... [is] shaped through a series of successive approximations, each made possible by selectively reinforcing certain responses and not others. Thus behavior is gradually brought closer and closer to the desired pattern [p. 71].

On our practice trips, I acutely observed the pupil's behavior in order to immediately reinforce approximations of correct behavior. Nonverbal cues that demonstrated understanding of component units were reinforced. In teaching a pupil to alight correctly from the bus, for example, behaviors such as widening the eyes or the pupil's moving to the edge of the seat when sighting and recognizing the proper landmark were approximations that indicated an appropriate response to a stimuli. When such approximate behaviors were observed, they were reinforced until the pupil learned the desired behavior of standing, ringing the buzzer, and walking up to the door to alight from the bus in response to the stimulus of sighting the landmark.

As the pupil began to appropriately perform each component unit, I then withdrew somewhat from the pupil and lessened the frequency of my reinforcement. In this way, the pupil was permitted to assert himself in performing the newly learned tasks. After a number of practice lessons, the pupil gradually began to lead the way through each component unit while I observed. My job then was to ensure for the pupil's safety.

Once the pupil was able to perform each component of his trip, I then withdrew almost completely. The pupil led the way, and I stayed as far away as possible, yet still remaining in a position to observe his performance. My function was to observe the pupil so that a decision could be made to determine if the pupil demonstrated the appropriate skills involved in using the public transit independently. I followed the pupil from a distance and attempted to keep from vision. This was accomplished by following the pupil on the bus, by following the bus via automobile, or by having another staff member observe the pupil on his route. After a number of successful repetitions of this process, an informed judgment could be made concerning the competence of a pupil to independently use the public transit.

Chapter 6

# THE MAKING OF AN INDEPENDENT———
# TRAVELER: A CASE STUDY————————

The world in which we live is not always safe, secure, and predictable. It does not always say 'please' or 'excuse me.' Every day that we wake up and live in the hours of that day, there is a possibility of being thrown up against a situation where we may have to risk everything, even our lives. This is the way the *real* world is. We must work to develop every human resource within us in order to prepare for these days. To deny any person their fair share of risk experiences is to further cripple them for healthy living.

Robert Perske
*The Principle of Normalization in Human Services*

IN order to clarify the five steps in teaching the skills involved in the independent use of the public transit, the following is a case study of Robert. For the past six years Robert, a sixteen-year-old Downe's syndrome pupil, has been enrolled in an inner city public school program for the trainable mentally retarded. Prior to orientation and mobility instruction, he was transported daily between home and the center via taxicab. As the result of specialized instruction, Robert has successfully learned to travel independently between home and the center via the public transit. At the time of this writing, Robert has been independently using the public transit daily for this trip during the past three years.

## ANALYZING THE SKILL

The goal was to teach Robert to travel daily the fifteen miles between his home and the center via the public transit. After consulting with his parents as well as with the transit authority, we established a safe and direct route for Robert to travel. In this route, Robert was required to take one bus into the downtown business district and then transfer to a second bus. The following chain of behaviors comprised the trip from the center to home:

S Identify bus-stop sign
↓
R Stand by the bus-stop sign

•

S Identify bus (16E)
↓
R Enter bus

•

S Face driver
↓
R Pay fare, ask for transfer

•

S Identify unoccupied seat
↓
R Sit down

•

S Identify landmark for alighting (music store)
↓
R Ring buzzer

•

S Door opens
↓
R Alight from bus

•

S Faced with music store
↓
R Turn left and walk until you approach typewriter store

•

S Identify typewriter store
↓
R Stand in front of typewriter store

•

S Identify second bus (77B)

R  Enter bus

•

S  Identify unoccupied seat
↓
R  Sit down

•

S  Identify landmark for alighting (ice cream stand)
↓
R  Ring buzzer

•

S  Face driver
↓
R  Give driver transfer slip

•

S  Face opened door
↓
R  Alight from bus

•

S  Faced with familiar neighborhood
↓
R  Walk home

The trip from home to the center consisted of the following chain of behaviors:

S  Identify bus-stop sign
↓
R  Stand by the bus-stop sign

•

S  Identify bus (77B)
↓
R  Enter bus

•

S  Face driver
↓
R  Pay fare, ask for transfer

•

S  Identify unoccupied seat

R  Sit down

•

S  Identify landmark for alighting (typewriter store)
↓
R  Ring buzzer

•

S  Door opens
↓
R  Alight from bus

•

S  Faced with typewriter store
↓
R  Turn right and walk until you come to music store

•

S  Identify music store
↓
R  Stand in front of music store

•

S  Identify second bus (16E)
↓
R  Enter bus

•

S  Identify unoccupied seat
↓
R  Sit down

•

S  Identify landmark for alighting (gas station)
↓
R  Ring buzzer

•

S  Face driver
↓
R  Give driver transfer slip

•

S  Face opened door

R Alight from bus

•

S Faced with familiar neighborhood

R Walk to the center

The above chain of behaviors was required to be learned in order for Robert to independently travel to and from the center. The next step was to assess Robert's entering behavior.

### ASSESSING THE ENTERING BEHAVIOR

Robert was identified as a candidate for orientation and mobility instruction because he demonstrated competence in the four requisite behaviors that had been established for candidacy. This decision was based on data collected from his classroom teachers, school specialists that were familiar with Robert, and my observation of and interaction with Robert.

The data depicted Robert as emotionally stable; while somewhat of an introvert, he was accepted by his peers as well as the staff. He was free of bizzare behaviors and seemed to deal appropriately with familiar and unfamiliar adults. He was able to follow directions and learn basic routines, and he achieved according to his ability level in the classroom. Robert was able to make action decisions and initiate movement. The teachers reported that at times his action decisions posed problems within the group setting; this behavior was described as stubbornness, but it did not seem to be a major problem. Robert was able to identify and discriminate red, yellow, and green colors and was able to indicate what these colors meant in a street-crossing situation. His speech was unintelligible to those that were not familiar with him; however, his receptive language ability permitted his appropriate response to instruction. He was not able to state his home address and phone number intelligibly and was not able to use a public pay phone.

As a result of an interview with his mother, further information was gathered. It was learned that Robert did not play unsupervised in his neighborhood. He did make small purchases at a local grocery with the help of a note from his mother; however, he had no understanding or competence of using money in these purchases. His family owned an automobile, and they rarely used the public transit system. Robert had little experience using the public bus with others, and he had never been on a public bus alone. The following is the Parent Interview Form used to gather the above information from his mother:

## PARENT INTERVIEW FORM

Name    Mrs. Robert Jones

Parent of   Robert Jones, Jr.

1. Does you child play unsupervised in your neighborhood?
   no, he is not permitted to play alone

2. How far is your child permitted to play away from home?
   the front porch

3. Does your child travel independently to a friend or relative's home?   no

4. Does your child travel independently and make purchases at a local business?   yes, he goes to the neighborhood grocery store, the owner of this store is a friend

5. Is your child able to handle money responsibly?   no, mother gives him a note with an envelope for the money

6. Does your family routinely use public transportation facilities?   no

7. Has your child used a public transit bus in your company?
   yes

   How often?   about five times a year when the car is not operating

8. Where has your child traveled by public transit while accom-

panied by others? __downtown__

How often? __rarely__

9. Does you child regularly use a public bus? __no__

For what purpose? _____

Comments __Mrs. Jones seemed quite anxious__

## ARRANGING FOR TRAINING IN
## THE COMPONENT UNITS

In Robert's case, training was arranged for three component units: (1) bus-numeral identification, (2) paying the fare, and (3) identification of landmarks for alighting from the bus. By learning these component units prior to his outdoor lessons, Robert would be better prepared to focus on the overall trip rather than have to dwell on specific components at that time.

First, flash cards and worksheets were used by Robert's classroom teacher to help Robert learn to identify the bus numerals of the two buses he would use in his travel route. Also, the two numerals were written in the corner of his classroom chalkboard to be used as a reminder and for quick review. As a result of the classroom teacher's instruction, Robert learned that the 16E was the bus that he would board at the center in order to travel to the downtown district, and the 77B was the bus he would use to travel to his home. For the trip from home to the center, Robert learned that he would board the 77B in his neighborhood and it would take him into downtown. Once downtown, he would transfer to the 16E, which would take him to the center. Robert learned to associate the 16E with the center and the 77B with his home. After this instruction, Robert was able to discriminate the bus numerals that he would use from a large set of other bus numerals. I was not certain that Robert was clear about the order in which he would ride the two buses, but it was of no significant importance at this point.

Secondly, Robert was given instruction in how to pay the fare. He was given a monthly bus pass, ten-cent tickets, and an identification card that he placed in his wallet; he was told to have the wallet on his person every day. Robert learned that in order to pay the bus fare he must display his bus pass, place one ten-cent ticket into the farebox, and ask for a transfer receipt. Due to Robert's unintelligible speech, he was instructed to point toward the transfer receipts in order to indicate his desire for one. This sequence was simulated many times in order for Robert to learn to perform it with ease and speed.

Third, Robert was given instruction in what landmark to look for that indicated when he should alight from the bus. The classroom teacher and I cut pictures from a magazine to represent the three alighting cues Robert would encounter: a music store, a typewriter store, and a gas station. These papers were posted on Robert's classroom bulletin board and were referred to numerous times during the outdoor instructional process.

## DESCRIBING AND DEMONSTRATING THE SKILL

This step was the beginning of outdoor instruction, where the pupil began use of the public transit on his designated travel route. I met Robert in the morning at the center after his arrival via his usual means, the taxicab. Robert checked into his homeroom; I directed him out of the building, and I pointed out the bus-stop sign that indicated where he would wait for his first bus. We stood by the bus-stop sign, facing the direction in which the bus would approach. In a short time, the bus appeared; Robert and I walked up to the curb to wait while the bus doors opened. I entered first, while Robert followed closely behind. I demonstrated the fare payment procedure by opening my wallet, displaying my bus pass, depositing my ten-cent ticket, and pointing to the transfer receipts. The bus driver understood this signal and responded by giving me one. Robert then was verbally coached through this process. I located two unoccupied seats as near to the front as possible; we sat down.

The landmark for alighting from the bus in the downtown district was a music store with a large neon guitar on the store's facade. Thereupon, I referred to it as the "guitar store." As we were riding the bus toward downtown, I reminded Robert to look out of the window for the "guitar store." When we approached this landmark, I stood up, rang the buzzer cord, and walked to the front of the bus; Robert followed. When the bus stopped and the doors opened, I alighted, with Robert following closely behind.

We made a left turn and walked down the street until a typewriter store was sighted. I led Robert to the typewriter store, and we looked in the store's window. I identified this store as one that sold typewriters; with our backs to this store's window, we stood to wait for the second bus. Numerous public buses approached this stop with a large number of people boarding and alighting from the bus; this transit stop was on a main transit line. As each bus approached, Robert was directed to the location of the route numerals on each bus. As we waited, about ten buses approached that were not the one required by Robert to travel home. As they approached, we looked at the route numerals on the bus, and I indicated that each did *not* read 77B. I mentioned that they were not the "right" bus, and if we boarded them, we would get lost.

Finally, the 77B arrived, and I identified it as the "right" bus that would transport us to Robert's neighborhood. We approached the curb and waited for the bus to pull up to the curb. When the doors opened, I entered with Robert following; again, we looked for unoccupied seats nearest the front and sat down. Similar to the procedure in the first bus, Robert was reminded to look out the window for our alighting landmark in his neighborhood; this was an ice cream store with which he was familiar.

Once we approached this landmark, I stood up and pointed

out the ice cream store. I explained that when we see it we must stand, ring the buzzer cord, and walk to the front of the bus. Once at the front of the bus, we waited as it pulled up to our stop. As the door opened, I gave the driver my transfer receipt; Robert did the same. For the first time in the trip, Robert appeared relaxed. Robert led the way to his home.

Since we called his mother prior to leaving, we stopped into Robert's home, for a visit. This was the last time we visited for it was not necessary to bother his mother every morning, and we did not have the luxury of the time that even a short visit would take.

We left his home and headed toward the bus stop where we would board the 77B for our return trip to the downtown district. To reach our bus stop, we had to cross a residential intersection that was controlled by traffic lights. Since this was the same intersection Robert had crossed many times in his travels to the neighborhood grocery, he seemed comfortable with it. He led the way as I evaluated his ability to cross this street. He started to cross appropriately, and I followed, while pointing out to him that he ought to be extra careful about cars turning in front of us from the parallel street. After crossing the street, I pointed out the bus-stop sign, and we began the wait for the bus for the return trip.

Soon the 77B bus appeared; we walked up to the curb facing the approaching bus; it stopped, and the doors opened. I pulled out my wallet, entered the bus, displayed my bus pass, put a ten-cent ticket in the farebox, and, while pointing toward the transfer receipts, I asked for one. Robert, right behind me, did the same, while I coached him through it. We found two unoccupied seats as near as possible to the front of the bus. While riding the bus into downtown, Robert was reminded that we would know when to get off the bus when we saw the typewriter store. Soon we entered the downtown business district, and the bus approached the typewriter store, which I pointed out. I told Robert that now I was going to stand, pull the buzzer cord, and walk to the front of the bus. As we alighted from the bus, we turned right and walked to the music store.

We identified the music store, looked in the window at the

for the bus that would transport us back to school. As numerous buses approached, I directed Robert to look at each bus numeral. Quite a few buses other than the 16E approached, but I mentioned that they were *not* a 16E, and we would *not* board them. When the 16E approached, I identified it as such and told Robert that this was the bus that would transport us to school. We walked up to the curb, and I boarded it, followed by Robert. We sat down and looked out the window as we watched the bus leave the business district on its way toward our center. Robert was familiar with the neighborhood surrounding our center, and soon we could see our final landmark, the gas station. We stood, I rang the buzzer cord, and handed the driver our transfer receipts as we alighted from the bus. Robert led the way to the center.

This trip was simply one of demonstration. Little was demanded of Robert at this point.

## PROVIDING FOR THE BASIC LEARNING CONDITIONS

Robert and I traveled through the complete travel route in each lesson between the center and Robert's home. While we proceeded through the travel route in a similar manner, the lessons differed only in the emphasis placed in each component unit of the route. The emphasis proceeded in a backward sequence, with the final component unit being the first focus for instruction. In Robert's case, the final component unit was locating his home. Once Robert demonstrated competence in a particular component unit, he then performed this component unit independently in subsequent lessons while I observed and followed from a distance.

## Lesson Two

The second lesson differed from the first only in that Robert was directed to lead the way through each component unit while I positioned myself closely behind him or at his side. Although Robert led the way through the complete travel route, I was close enough to give him verbal direction and support; in these early lessons, he was totally dependent on my direction. In subsequent lessons, I was able to follow further away from him as he began to gain the competence and confidence to deal with each component unit of the travel route.

### Lesson Three

After the first two lessons, Robert appeared to relax somewhat after the initial anxiety of being away from the center; little was demanded of him, and he seemed to be enjoying our daily trips. Since he was familiar with his home neighborhood where he alighted from the bus, he was able to lead me from the bus to his home without my direction. Thus he entered the instructional process with competence in the final component unit.

In this third lesson, he also demonstrated beginning competence in giving the driver the transfer receipt and alighting from the bus near his home. The next component unit that precedes these two final units, identifying the landmark for alighting in his home neighborhood (the ice cream store), was the next focus for instruction.

### Lesson Four

In the first three lessons, I took the initiative to identify the ice cream store in his neighborhood; upon sighting this landmark, I directed Robert to ring the buzzer cord that indicated to the bus driver that we wished to alight from the bus. In this fourth lesson, I explained to Robert that it was now his responsibility to identify this landmark and to initiate the behavior to alight from the bus. I explained that the bus would stop near his home only if we ring the buzzer cord. Furthermore, I added that unless we rang the buzzer cord, the bus would continue past his bus stop, and we would pass his neighborhood and be lost. This was explained to Robert prior to, during, and repeated subsequent to this fourth lesson.

As we approached his neighborhood, Robert became somewhat tense; his body tightened up, and he sat more toward the edge of his seat. When the ice cream store was in sight, his eyes widened, but he did not initiate movement toward the buzzer cord. He turned his head toward me as if to say "Aren't you going to lead the way?"

I perceived the following behavior as being an approximation of the behavior required to alight from the bus: Robert becoming increasingly tense as we approached his neighborhood, his sitting on the edge of the seat once the bus approached the ice cream store, and his eyes widening as he saw the ice cream store. This indicated to me that he recognized his landmark, and that he knew he was required to do something in order to get off the bus. This was the beginning step; at least he seemed aware that some response was required of him. Accordingly I reinforced him. I said, "Yes, now you must stand, ring the buzzer cord, and walk up front." I waited until he did this and followed him up to the driver where we gave him our transfer receipts and alighted from the bus. I told him that it appeared to me that he had identified the ice cream store, but that the next time he must react by ringing the buzzer cord without seeking my approval.

## Lesson Five

In this lesson, Robert exhibited the same approximation of behaviors as we entered his neighborhood. He sat on the edge of his seat, and he appeared somewhat tense. When he sighted the ice cream store, his eyes widened, and it seemed that internally he was saying, "That's it!" But he did not move toward the buzzer cord; he only looked toward me. I responded by saying that he must now ring the buzzer. He did, and we alighted from the bus.

## Lesson Six

Again the focus of instruction for this lesson was the component unit of alighting from the bus near Robert's home. Robert and I reviewed the situation over and over again. "When you see the ice cream store, you must stand up immediately and ring the buzzer cord," he was told. When he sighted the ice cream store on this trip, he raised his hand to the buzzer cord without ringing it. "Yes, very good," I said. "Now ring the buzzer." He did.

### Lesson Seven

After considerably more verbal review, Robert began watching for the ice cream store. When he sighted it, he raised his hand to the buzzer cord and rang the buzzer. Robert was reinforced, and we stood up and alighted from the bus. Robert demonstrated competence in this component unit.

### Lesson Eight

Up to this point, Robert demonstrated competence in the following component units (listed in reverse sequence): walking from the point where he alighted from the bus to his home, paying the fare as he alighted from the bus, ringing the buzzer cord to alert the bus driver that he wanted to alight, and sighting the landmark which indicated it was the appropriate time to alight from the bus. These component units were performed independently by Robert while I observed from a distance and reinforced him for these behaviors.

The next focus for instruction was the identification of the 77B, the bus that he would board in the downtown district for his trip home. We stood in front of the typewriter store; as each bus approached, I asked Robert if that particular bus was the one that would take us to his home.

This questioning was done with neutral intonation, not giving Robert any verbal cue as to whether it was the correct bus approaching or not. In addition, I was conscious of not providing nonverbal body or facial cues. I had to be careful not to behave differently, move my body differently, or present facial expressions that would communicate to Robert that a bus that approached was his correct bus or incorrect bus.

Robert appeared to have benefited from his previous classroom instruction in this component unit as well as the eight previous repetitions of this travel route. When I asked Robert if each bus that approached was his, he responded by saying "No." The sixth bus to approach was the 77B. He said, "Yes," but just stood there. I responded by saying, "Well, what do you do now?" He pointed toward the bus, paused, and then walked toward the bus door, and we boarded.

### Lesson Nine

When we arrived at the typewriter store in this lesson, I did not ask Robert about each bus that approached. I just stood and let Robert initiate the identification and boarding of the bus. Robert demonstrated competence in this component unit.

The next focus for instruction was for Robert to face the music store, turn left, walk to the typewriter store, and stand in front of the typewriter store. As we alighted from our first bus, Robert was instructed to find the typewriter store. Instead of turning left, he turned right and started to walk. We walked until he came to the next intersection and Robert knew something was wrong; I stood behind him, waiting until Robert made a decision. He turned back, and we passed the bus stop and walked to the typewriter store. Robert smiled, and I explained that the reason we got into trouble was that we turned the wrong way when we alighted from the bus. Although Robert made a turning error, he was able to recover from the error on his own.

### Lesson Ten

As in the previous lesson, the focus for instruction was for Robert to demonstrate competence in walking from the music store to the typewriter store. Robert and I alighted from the first bus at the music store. He paused. He looked to the right and then to the left; he turned left and walked toward the typewriter store. When he arrived to the point where he had previously waited in front of the typewriter store, he found a uniformed Salvation Army person who had set up a table from which he was singing hymns. Robert walked up to the table and positioned himself in front of the table, for this is where he was accustomed to wait for his second bus. That Robert would stand in front of the collection basket seemed to anger the Salvation Army person. Robert seemed confused, but he did move a few feet to the side to satisfy the Salvation Army person. While moving, he still remained in the area to success-fully board his second bus, the 77B. Mastery of this unit was achieved.

## Summary

The instruction continued in this manner; each daily lesson provided experience for Robert in traveling the whole route. Early in the instructional process, the final component units were the focus of instruction. However, Robert also was experiencing the early component units, and as the instruction progressed, the component units were learned more quickly by Robert. He learned that he must act on his own while I followed his direction. By his fifteenth lesson, Robert had demonstrated competence in the total trip. In lessons, fifteen through eighteen, I followed him from a distance to evaluate his competence. After the eighteenth lesson, Robert was certified as an independent traveler.

Chapter 7

# RESULTS, OUTCOMES, AND _____
# PRESCRIPTIONS_____

> There must be something the matter with him
>   because he would not be acting as he does
>     unless there was
>   therefore he is acting as he is
>   because there is something the matter with him.
>
> R. D. Laing<br>*Knots*

IN four years, 115 pupils have learned to travel safely and independently to and from the center via the public transit. These pupils, who, prior to their orientation and mobility instruction, were transported daily to the center in taxicabs and vans, learned to initiate and to be responsible for their own daily travel. Not only did they demonstrate independent travel skills, but, equally important, the pupils practiced safe travel techniques. Although parents had expressed many fears for the safety of the pupils, there have been no incidents that resulted in harm to any pupil. There were no reported incidents of sexual molestation, kidnapping, or accidents, all of which were the major concern of parents, as reported by Cortazzo and Sansone (1969). There were occasions, however, where pupils became disoriented for a few hours, but these incidents occurred early in the pupil's independent travel, and no harm resulted from these experiences. The program proved to be both safe and feasible.

## SHORT-TERM FOLLOW-UP

The following is a short-term analysis of the current status of the 115 pupils who learned orientation and mobility skills:

Currently traveling independently to the center via
 public transit .................................... 60
Currently attending the center, but are *not* traveling
 independently via the public transit ............... 3
Currently traveling independently to sheltered workshop
 employment via the public transit ................. 32
Currently traveling independently to competitive employment via the public transit.............. 2
Transferred to another school district and are *not*
 traveling independently via public transit .......... 7
Transferred to another school district and is traveling
 independently via the public transit ............... 1
Withdrew from public school and are unemployed .... <u>10</u>

Pupils who learned to travel independently via the
 public transit ....................................115

Sixty pupils are currently traveling successfully to the center
via the public transit. Once these pupils were able to demonstrate successfully the negotiation of their travel route, there
were no subsequent orientation problems, other major problems, or accidents.

However, there are three pupils who are currently attending
the center who, while having demonstrated competence in independent travel, have nevertheless discontinued use of the
public transit and are transported once again by taxicab. The
families of two of these pupils moved to a different neighborhood and denied the center permission to have their children
reoriented in order to continue their use of the public transit.
The third pupil, after being successful in independent travel,
demonstrated inappropriate behavior which indicated a lack of
emotional readiness. Her independent travel was terminated. In
addition to the sixty pupils currently traveling to the center and
the three who have learned independent travel skills but are not
applying them, there are also thirty-two pupils who have grad-
uated from the center program and are currently employed at
sheltered workshops. They were reoriented to a route from their
home to their work site and are successfully traveling independently to work via the public transit. Two other graduates are

placed in competitive job sites, and they also are continuing to travel independently. Eight pupils who were independent travelers at the center have transferred to other public school programs, but seven of these eight are no longer permitted by their new school district to travel via the public transit. One pupil of the eight, who transferred out of the state, is still using his independent travel skills. Finally, ten other pupils who were traveling independently to the center have withdrawn from public school, and there is little available data to determine if they have continued to use their orientation and mobility skills.

## OUTCOMES

The orientation and mobility instruction program for the trainable mentally retarded pupils in the Pittsburgh Public Schools proved to be safe and feasible and one that has resulted in a number of significant outcomes to help reduce dependency of the school district's trainable mentally retarded pupils. One outcome was that pupils were provided an opportunity for interaction with normal societal contacts. Another was that they learned a skill that will have direct future utility. They also developed an improved self-concept. Furthermore, pupils learned to be responsible for arriving at the center on time and learned dressing skills. Finally, the program resulted in a reduction of transportation costs for the school district. Let us now examine these outcomes.

First, orientation and mobility instruction significantly changed the daily routine of 115 pupils by providing them with the opportunity to engage in the normalized activity of being responsible for their daily travel via the public transit; the program provided them with the opportunity to interact with normal societal contacts. Wolf Wolfensberger stresses the importance of societal integration of the handicapped saying:

> If we are serious about working for the goal of preparing a person toward independence and normative functioning, then we must prepare him to function in the context of the ordinary societal contact which he is expected to have and to handle adaptively in the future [p. 45].

Admittedly, our public school program for trainable mentally retarded pupils as it is now structured, does not permit our pupils to function during the school day in "the context of ordinary societal contacts" to the degree that Wolfensberger proposes. Our pupils are segregated in a "special" center. I am not in the position to change this; however, each of the 115 pupils who learned independent travel skills, at least in daily travel to and from the center, has the opportunity to function in the "context of the ordinary societal contacts which he is expected to have and to handle adaptively in the future" [p. 45].

Secondly, orientation and mobility instruction enabled pupils to learn skills that will have direct future utility. While the skills learned in orientation and mobility are taught in the context of the one route from home to school, they are nevertheless applicable and transferable to travel in other diverse routes. There is evidence of pupils' being able to apply travel skills learned on one route to another route within the community. As mentioned above, thirty-two pupils are currently traveling to workshop employment sites. While these pupils received help in reorientation to the new route, other pupils learned diverse routes on their own. Pupils spent time downtown "looking around," having coffee, and shopping before they continued on their way to or from the center. Some pupils learned routes to a friend's house and have visited them after school and on weekends. Other pupils did minor shopping for their parents. A few others learned routes to the center other than the one in which they were originally instructed and, for various reasons, prefer to use the alternate route. Those pupils who diverted from their learned route, for whatever reason, demonstrated a higher level of travel skill. But this was only possible by learning the skills and developing confidence in the one route to the center.

Third, those pupils who became independent travelers gave indications of perceiving themselves more as independent young adults rather than dependent children; they developed an improved self-concept. One stigma the pupils suffered from prior to orientation and mobility instruction was of being required to be picked up and transported daily on "special" vehicles. In the morning, while others of their age were walking to school, waiting for the public bus, or even waiting for their "normal" school bus, our pupils were being picked up at their doorsteps. Our pupils were sensitive to this stigma, and it conveyed a meaningful message to the neighborhood and indeed to our pupils; a message that our pupils were different, undesirable, and inferior. Use of the public transit tended to somewhat undo this one stigma.

Subsequent to success in independent travel, positive changes have been observed in our pupils. As I reported in my earlier article (1974):

> There was a strong indication of feelings of achievement among the independent travelers. Their realization of an adult function greatly enhanced a more positive self concept and this attitude permeated their behavior and performance in other aspects of the school curriculum [p. 72].

I recognize that such statements attributing positive attitude change are subjective and may be untenable to those who require empirical data. Such observations may be vulnerable to critics who might ask how the variable of learning independent travel was isolated from natural growth, maturation, and maturity. Nevertheless, such attitude and behavior change has been attested to by myself, classroom teachers, workshop supervisors, and parents.

To explain the observed attitude change, I facetiously tell people that I have developed a hypothesis in this regard. Let us assume that feelings of worth and positive self-concept are correlated to body gait, and we can measure self-concept by posture. If we could measure the distance from a pupil's chin to the pavement prior to orientation and mobility instruction and then measure the distance from the same two points after success in the use of the public transit, we would find an increased distance to a significant degree in the final test. This would demonstrate that our pupil's gait has improved, and we could make the assumption that this was the result of increased pride and feelings of worth since the pupil became an independent traveler. To be serious again, it has been observed that our pupils do feel good about their independent travel, they demonstrate improved posture, they are proud of their accomplishment, and they have improved behavior and performance in other aspects of the center's program subsequent to success in independent travel.

Fourth, as the result of the orientation and mobility program, pupils have had the opportunity to learn and be responsible for arriving at the center each morning on time. I can recall, prior to the development of the orientation and mobility program, observing lessons on "getting to work on time." The teacher would lecture in the classroom on the importance and sanctity of arriving to work on time, and the pupils would listen to a cassette tape or watch a film strip with the same message. And yet, in the context of the school program, were the pupils ever given the responsibility to arrive on time? No, they were being picked up daily by a taxicab, and to make the point even more absurd, the cabs were inevitably late. In contrast to this, the pupils at our center who use the public transit are required upon arrival every morning to "punch in" on a time clock. In this way, we have an accurate record of the arrival times of each pupil. If we notice that a particular person is consistently tardy, the problem then can be recognized, and efforts can be made to modify this behavior. By using such a procedure with pupils who learn independent travel skills, we were able to gather evidence that a particular pupil was reliable in his arrival time. By the time a pupil graduates and is placed in a vocational setting, he has learned the valuable work-related behavior of arriving to work on time. Obviously this behavior cannot be taught in a classroom, but it was a valuable outcome of the orientation and mobility program.

Learning skills in dressing appropriately for weather conditions is the fifth significant outcome of the orientation and mobility program. When pupils were riding the taxicab to the center, there was little concern for appropriate dress. The pupils were just not exposed to the weather while being chauffered from their home doorstep to the center's doorstep. I have seen pupils wearing one light jacket throughout the entire cold Pittsburgh winter. If it rained, it did not matter, because the cab would pull right in front of the door that led to the center. In contrast to this, inappropriate choice of clothing while using the public transit brings harsh penalties if it becomes quite cold or if a rainstorm develops. The weather elements shaped the behavior of the independent travelers. They learned when to wear boots, gloves, or scarves, or when to carry an umbrella. In many cases, pupils had to be instructed in how to independently use an umbrella and how to carry it safely. By using the public transit, pupils learned valuable dressing skills that are important requisites for an independent working citizen.

Finally, the orientation and mobility program significantly reduced transportation costs to the school district. All four hundred trainable mentally retarded pupils who attended our center were transported daily to the center via taxicabs or leased vans prior to the establishment of the orientation and mobility program. This policy reached the highest level of absurdity by including even those adolescent pupils who lived down the street or around the corner from the center. The cost of providing transportation to all the pupils was and still is a significant part of the yearly budget for programs serving the mentally retarded and all other disability groups. It has been estimated that the per capita cost of providing this service is six dollars per day per pupil. When comparing the daily cost for travel to and from the center via the public transit, it becomes quite clear that a significant savings can result by having pupils use the latter mode of daily transportation. The school district saved five dollars per day for every day traveled by a pupil on the public transit. There is a hundred-dollar-per-month savings (a twenty-day school month) incurred by one pupil traveling on the public transit in lieu of a taxicab, and a thousand-dollar-per-year savings (ten-month school year) by having one pupil travel on the public transit. After fifty pupils have learned to travel independently, simple arithmetic tells us that the transportation budget can be reduced by $50,000 per year. This significant budget reduction occurred with only one additional staff member, the orientation and mobility instructor, with a salary between $10,000 and $16,000. In the fourth year of the program, a second instructor was added, but still the savings are quite apparent. As I stated in my previous article (1974):

In addition to being of significant value to the pupil's growth toward independent living, the program is economically self-financing [p. 72].

## PRESCRIPTIONS FOR CLASSROOM TEACHERS

With the knowledge that many mentally retarded pupils are capable of independent travel and that there is an important relationship between expectations and performance, in-service teachers must take an introspective look at their own expectations for their pupils. Teachers must go through a consciousness-raising process of their own, and if they are willing and able, they can begin to communicate these raised expectations to those pupils within their classroom.

While I am speaking here of an attitudinal change on part of the teacher, it can be manifested through curriculum modification, change, and innovation in the types of skill-learning and other experiences provided for pupils. Teachers should teach academic skills that have been identified as requisites for independent travel. Although teachers may believe they are already teaching these skills, they must reexamine how they are taught and relate the teaching of these skills to use of the public transit.

Teachers also should expand the number of community experiences for their class. Instead of requisitioning a school bus to transport the class on field trips, the public transit system, with a few modifications such as additional parent or volunteer chaperones, can be used to provide more realistic societal contact. Efforts should be made to maintain small group size so that the pupils are manageable and so that the community interaction will be more meaningful.

Furthermore, the teacher should examine the classroom atmosphere with regards to the opportunity provided for pupils to initiate movement and make decisions. The opportunity should be provided for pupils to make decisions and initiate movement within the daily classroom routine. There must be opportunity for gradual independence of movement within the room, building, and immediate school neighborhood. With revised expectations communicated to pupils, classroom teachers can play a vital role in the future travel independence of their pupils.

In addition, classroom teachers must make efforts to communicate these raised expectations to parents. There are many opportunities for teachers, when discussing a pupil's future with parents, to include the goal of independent travel in such conferences. Parents must learn that independent travel is a feasible goal for many handicapped persons.

Finally, classroom teachers must ask themselves: If many pupils can independently use the public transit when we thought they were not capable, are there other skills that handicapped persons can perform that we presently think they cannot perform?

## PRESCRIPTIONS FOR DIRECTORS OF PROGRAMS

Risk is the name of the game. Implementation of an orientation and mobility program involves the undertaking of a significant risk on the part of program directors (public schools, sheltered workshops, activity centers, group homes, rehabilitation centers, state institutions, etc.) for handicapped persons. Unlike other program innovations, independent travel permits pupils to function beyond the tight perimeter of supervision that has been characteristic of traditional programs for the handicapped. As the result there exist many inherent potential inconveniences and problems: pupils may arrive late for school, pupils may arrive home late and parents may call to ask why, pupils may lose their bus passes, pupils may get lost, pupils may behave inappropriately on the public transit, etc. At worst, there always exists the possibility that physical harm may come to the pupils. Nevertheless, if directors of programs are sincerely interested in reducing dependence and providing normalized learning experiences for handicapped persons, they must accept the inherent risks and make a commitment to include orientation and mobility instruction as an integral part of their training process.

Once program directors decide to make the commitment to develop an orientation and mobility program, they have an important responsibility in selecting the staff members to plan and implement the program. Programmatic success and the minimization of risk can be the beneficiary of judicious selection of staff. The staff chosen should have some of the following qualities: experience with the population, familiarity with normalization principles, maturity and sound judgment, and communication skills to relate with the parents, colleagues, and pupils. The following elaborate on these qualities.

While these qualities are not intended to be all-inclusive, they do provide some guidelines for staff selection. First, staff should have experience with the types of pupils that will be candidates for instruction. By having experience with the population, it is expected that staff will have an understanding of the abilities and limitations of the population. In addition, staff that are selected should be those who choose to be working with the population, and who feel comfortable in their presence. Second, staff should possess the assumptions inherent in the normalization process as outlined in Chapter 2 in the sections by Conant (1976). Third, staff should possess the qualities of maturity and sound judgment, since they will be required to make crucial decisions in the instructional process. The staff will be required to possess the delicate balance in judgment between permissiveness that will allow pupils to assert their independence and care for the pupil's safety. Finally, staff should have communication skills that will enable them to relate appropriately with others. A key responsibility of the orientation and mobility instructor is to gain the support and trust of parents, colleagues, and pupils. These qualities can provide the framework for staff selection.

In summation, program directors are in a pivotal role to exercise leadership in the establishment of orientation and mobility programs. The success achieved in the first few pioneering programs has provided the impetus for future implementation. Program directors must now accept the risk and make the commitment for programming that will result in greater growth and independence for mentally retarded citizens. Where else can program directors find a program that results in a significant cost reduction in services and yet provides the opportunity for mentally retarded persons to grow beyond past expectations?

## PRESCRIPTIONS FOR UNIVERSITY ORIENTATION AND MOBILITY PROGRAMS FOR THE BLIND

Since 1960, both undergraduate and graduate university programs have been established to train professionals to teach orientation and mobility skills to blind persons. Students in these programs receive general and special education courses as well as courses specific to blindness, such as Dynamics of Human Behavior Related to Blindness, Medical Aspects of Blindness, Psychological Aspects of Blindness, etc. There is a practicum in orientation and mobility where students must learn personal mastery, under the blindfold, of precane skills and mobility techniques with the long cane. Also, students are required to do extensive observations of instruction and perform a supervised internship with blind persons in various settings (public schools, private schools, rehabilitation centers, etc.).

One implication of the success of orientation and mobility programs for the sighted handicapped persons is that university programs may wish to consider the broadening of the scope of their curriculum to include courses that deal with other disability groups, thus creating internships where students would teach a variety of handicapped persons. Perhaps university programs should take a step further and develop a curriculum that would prepare instructors to teach orientation and mobility skills to those of all disability groups. This generic approach to an orientation and mobility university curriculum would not be limited to categories (blindness, mental retardation, physically handicapped, etc.), but would study the needs for travel instruction and develop strategies for teaching pupils of all disability areas. This would be consistent with the general trend toward decategorization of disability groups. Also, more and more persons who require special education or rehabilitation, professionals are discovering, do not fit neatly in the traditional categories. As witness to this, many university programs training professionals to teach multiply handicapped persons are emerging across the country.

One practical outcome of this type of university training is that graduates would have greater flexibility in locating employment. For example, there are many small or medium-sized public school districts that do not have enough blind persons to justify the hiring of a full-time orientation and mobility instructor. But if the orientation and mobility instructor has experience and competencies in working with other disability groups in addition to blind pupils, then the hiring of a full-time orientation and mobility instructor might be justified.

### PRESCRIPTIONS FOR PARENTS

The implications for parents as the result of the success of orientation and mobility programs for sighted mentally retarded persons are clear. As I have discussed many times throughout this book — and it is so important that I'll mention it again — parents also must raise their expectations in regards to independent travel as a feasible goal for their child. This is possible with the help of teachers, counselors, and parent organizations. Parents must be informed as to what part they can play to provide their child with important early learning experiences. Parents must realize that they must give their child as many normalized experiences as possible.

Whenever possible, parents should take their child with them as they travel about in the community. If parents normally use the public transit, they should bring their child with them. Parents should permit the child to lead the way, identify the correct bus, pay their own fare, decide where to sit, make the decision when to alight from the bus, and ring the buzzer that tells the driver when a passenger wishes to alight. While the child leads the way, the parent should follow to supervise this activity, make corrections, and reward their child's appropriate behavior. If the public transit is not the normal mode of travel for the family, the parents should make efforts to use it occasionally in lieu of the family car. Also, parents should permit their child to use the public transit with responsible siblings.

In addition to providing their child with experiences using the public transit, parents should permit their child to be more independent within their neighborhood. They should permit their child to play outside with other children in the neighborhood. Yes, it may be difficult to do, and the child may be on the receiving end of ridicule or harassment, but handicapped children, like normal children, must learn to cope with such situations and should be permitted to do so. Parents should give their child responsibilities to make small purchases in the community, deposit mail in the mailbox, deliver messages to neighbors, return borrowed sugar, and even to have their own paper route. If parents can permit their child to gain these types of valuable experiences, they will be taking a giant step toward travel independence for their child.

With the knowledge that independent travel is a feasible goal for many handicapped persons, parents must lobby for the establishment of orientation and mobility programs. This is an important implication. Parents must direct the power of their parent organizations to make certain that their children will have the opportunity to benefit from an orientation and mobility program. Parent organizations have demonstrated their impact in being responsible in the past for significant change, and they can be successful in being the impetus for orientation and mobility program development.

Chapter 8

# A DAY IN THE LIFE

Well, let me tell you a story
of a man named Charlie
on a tragic and fateful day.
He put ten cents in his pocket
kissed his wife and family
went to ride on the M. T. A.

Well, did he ever return?
No, he never returned
and his fate is still unlearned.
What a pity!
He may ride forever on the streets of Boston.
He's the man who never returned.

Kingston Trio
"M. T. A."

CONCOMITANT with the orientation and
mobility program were problems, humorous moments, fail-
ures, successes, disappointments, and joys. This chapter is a
potpourri of incidents that have occurred during orientation
and mobility instruction and as a result of our many pupils
becoming independent travelers. These anecdotes may be
helpful to the reader and may provide insight to the orientation
and mobility process which in turn will complement earlier
chapters.

## Louis

Louis was a difficult case. It was a long battle, but after four
weeks of intensive instruction, Louis appeared ready to travel
independently on the public transit. According to orientation
and mobility jargon, Louis was ready for his first "solo flight."
Louis was permitted to travel home via public transit at the end

of the school day. He boarded the public bus in front of the school building at 3:05 PM, and his estimated time of arrival at home was 4:00 PM. At 4:45, I received a phone call from Louis's mother, who anxiously stated that Louis had not yet arrived. I suggested that we wait a little longer. Hesitantly she agreed, but at 5:15 PM, she called again. Louis was not home. I called the center principal, the missing persons bureau, and the transit authority to seek assistance in locating Louis. I gave them a description of him, and they said they would do everything possible to find him. At this point, all we could do was wait.

At 8:15 PM, the transit authority called to say that they found Louis and that he was on a bus that was returning to the bus garage. I put on my coat and drove down to the bus station to wait for him. It was a dark, cold evening with a brisk wind, and rain was pelting against the pavement as I waited outside the garage for Louis. I could see a bus approaching, and it pulled up to where I was standing. Louis was on it. Later we learned that he had been riding for four hours on a bus that he incorrectly boarded. As Louis alighted from the bus, I asked what had happened. In a cool, unemotional tone, Louis explained, "I got hung up in traffic."

After a remedial lesson, Louis went on to become a successful independent traveler.

## Willie

Willie spent the first fourteen years of his life as a resident in a state institution for the mentally retarded. After his fifteenth birthday, he was discharged from the institution, placed in a group home, and enrolled at the center. Willie was highly verbal and, for our population, an above-average pupil. As a result of the orientation and mobility instruction, he learned to travel independently via the public transit. One day, his group home counselor inquired about Willie's being instructed to travel to the university section of Pittsburgh, an area unfamiliar to Willie, so that he would be able to attend a weekly post-school counseling session with his state counselor. I agreed to familiarize Willie with this section of town so that he could attend those sessions. Willie learned quickly, and after two lessons, he demonstrated travel competence. Willie was obviously excited with the prospect of traveling to his "meeting," which was his term for his weekly counseling session. The day after Willie made his first independent trip to his meeting, I stopped him in the hall of the center. "Did your first trip go alright?"

"I had one problem," he responded.

"What was that?" I queried.

"Well, when I got off the bus, I became confused. So I walked down the street, and I stopped some man. I asked, 'Do you know where the meeting is?' He didn't. So I walked more, and I saw this lady. I asked her, 'Do you know where the meeting is?' She didn't either. So you know, I just figured I had to find it myself. And you know I walked around a bit, and I found the meeting myself."

### Big Ed

Ed looked like a mouthbreathing wrestler cast into the role of villain. He stood a full 6 feet 3 inches tall and weighed 240 pounds, his abdominal muscles stretching into a grotesque pot belly. His hair was always closely cropped, similar to the haircuts required in basic military training programs, and he had large protruding ears. But his manner and personality were the antithesis of his appearance; he was a friendly, pleasant, and well-adjusted pupil. I recall quite clearly the apprehensive double takes and stares that were directed toward Ed by pedestrians and public transit riders during orientation and mobility instruction. Ed learned to travel independently and, at the time of this writing, has been traveling independently for three years. One of my most rewarding moments occurred a short time ago when I happened to be downtown after the end of the school day. From across the street, I saw a familiar face in the window of a tobacco store; it was Ed. My first thought was that Ed was lost or confused, but soon I saw him come out the door, and in his hand was a magazine. He waited for a green light, crossed the street, and walked toward me. I asked Ed what he was doing, and in his barely intelligible speech he explained that he had just purchased a magazine. He held it out for me to see. I stood there in total disbelief; on the cover were two female wrestlers, one tearing off the bra of the other. I was delighted that Ed had strayed from his travel route home to stop to make a purchase. And totally overwhelming was the idea that he was coherent enough to break away from his pattern a second time before reaching his destination — the bus stop — to speak to a friend.

## Reggie

In order to proceed to his second bus, Reggie was required to walk a seven-block zig-zag pattern through downtown Pittsburgh. Since Reggie had difficulty maintaining orientation on this component of the trip, many repetitions of this route were required. One day as we were practicing, Reggie complained, "Mr. Laus, I gotta go to bathroom."

"You'll have to wait a few minutes, Reggie. We have to find a restroom."

About a half block later Reggie's voice trembled, "Gotta go!"

I tried to calm him, hoping my tone of voice would ease his tension. "The restroom is only two blocks away. You can hold it, Reggie."

By now, Reggie had begun the quivering leg movements of the Charleston, and in his embarrassment he cried out, "Oh, here it comes!"

And it did. The right leg of his trousers was soaked, urine dripping from his cuffs to the pavement. "What now? What now?" he cried.

We continued on our way to the bus stop. I directed Reggie to stand in the direct sunlight, and we waited for the next bus back to the center.

## Curtis

Curtis went to a sheltered workshop for a placement interview. He was standing in a hallway talking with one of the evaluators, who was a 6'6", two hundred-sixty-pound National Football League offensive guard. Just then, to Curtis' surprise, a blind person with a guide dog quickly paced toward him. Curtis screamed and, in a desperate charge, knocked down and literally ran over the professional football player. It seemed that Curtis suffered from a phobia of dogs. As a result, a psychologist worked at desensitizing him to his fear. Parathetically, it seemed also that this football player/off-season vocational evaluator never did recover from his encounter with Curtis. During the subsequent training camp, he was cut from his squad and now is a full-time vocational evaluator.

### *Ken*

At the bus stop, Ken was not able to react quickly enough to approaching buses. He knew his bus number and was able to discriminate "his" bus number from others on worksheets and flashcards, but out on the street, he took too much time to make the decision. By the time he decided that a particular bus was one that he wished to board, it was gone. This problem was communicated to his classroom teacher. The next day, while passing Ken's classroom, I noticed something peculiar occurring. All of Ken's classmates were holding large signs above their heads and were marching in a procession past Ken. Upon closer examination, I learned that each member of the class was pretending to be a bus moving past Ken, so that he could practice the identification of moving buses.

### *Donald*

Donald was ready for his first "solo flight." He left the center on the 3:15 PM bus, and he was required to alight in front of a prominent department store in downtown Pittsburgh. From this point, he was to walk a few blocks to board a second bus that would take him to his neighborhood. His expected time of arrival at home was 4:15 PM. At 4:16 PM, Donald's mother called and said that Donald had not yet arrived home. I explained that it was premature at this point to be overly concerned. She reluctantly agreed. At 4:45 PM, she called again and was quite apprehensive. Again, my suggestion was that we wait a while longer. Soon I received another call from Donald's mother, and it was obvious that as time progressed, her anxiety heightened. I told her that we ought to wait until 6:00 PM, and then, if Donald was not home, we would take some action. At 5:45, she called to report that Donald had arrived home safely via the public transit.

Since Donald's speech was unintelligible, we later pieced together an explanation of what had occurred. Donald became distracted and did not alight at the department store. Apparently, he remained on the bus until it made its long loop through gradually increasing rush-hour traffic. The second time he passed the department store, he recognized his landmark and alighted from the bus. He walked the necessary few blocks, boarded his second bus, and arrived safely home. This was the first and last delay for Donald.

### Ruth Lynn

As the result of orientation and mobility instruction, Ruth Lynn learned to be an independent traveler. After about a week of successful travel to the center via the public transit, she did not arrive at the center. Her mother was notified, and she said that her daughter had left the house at 7:30 AM, apparently destined for the center. After a period of time, I got in my car and proceeded to look for Ruth Lynn. The search was in vain. At 2:15 PM, Ruth Lynn arrived at the center. We learned that Ruth Lynn did some sightseeing and shopping that day. She was accustomed to shopping in the downtown business area with her mother on Saturdays, and with her newly discovered independence, she decided to shop and sightsee on her own.

### Tom

Two divergent views were expressed when I first approached Tom's parents to seek their permission for Tom to receive orientation and mobility instruction. His mother believed that he was incapable of learning to use the public transit and that it was too dangerous for him to try, while his father insisted that Tom was capable and should receive instruction. After a lengthy family "discussion," the father's viewpoint prevailed, and Tom began orientation and mobility instruction.

After two weeks of instruction, Tom was ready for his "solo flight." He left the center at 3:00 PM, bound for home via the public transit, but by 6:30 PM, he had not arrived. His father notified the police and every public official with whom he was acquainted (which was an impressive number). Relatives on both sides of the family came over to Tom's house to join the search party. While in the presence of a houseful of relatives, Tom's parents engaged in a verbal battle, his mother initiating the first blow with an "I told you so!" They finally decided to go out in the community to search for Tom. At 9:30 PM, Tom was found sitting on a bench in downtown Pittsburgh. The next day, Tom's father came storming into the center. He asked me if I fought well. I said I didn't. He sat down and vented his anger. He called me many names that morning, the kindest being "incompetent." He insisted that I prematurely let his son ride the public bus. After he aired his feelings, he settled down, and I was able to talk. I explained that Tom was not prematurely permitted to travel independently, for he had demonstrated competence in the travel route. Furthermore, I suggested that there could have been numerous, unaccountable reasons as to why he became disoriented. It was my opinion that Tom did not need further instruction but needed another chance to demonstrate his travel competence. His father consented. The next day his "solo flight" was successful, and Tom has since traveled independently to the center on his own without a further incident.

### Emily

For three weeks, Emily demonstrated competence in independent travel. One morning during the fourth week, Emily did not arrive at the center at her usual time. We became concerned and called her home. Her mother reported that she had left that morning at her usual time. Four hours later, Emily was found on the wrong bus. This was perplexing because Emily had excellent numeral discrimination skills, and she was alert enough not to board an unfamiliar bus. We had difficulty learning from Emily what had occurred, due to her unintelligible speech. After some investigation, we learned how Emily boarded the incorrect bus, and why she remained on that bus for four hours. Emily had boarded the correct bus, but it broke down. Apparently, the driver transferred all the passengers onto another bus that traveled into town, but via a route unfamiliar to Emily. Since Emily had learned to only alight at a particular restaurant in town, and the bus did not pass that landmark, Emily rode the incorrect bus for four hours while waiting for it to pass her appointed alighting point.

## Sam

Sam was a difficult case. He seemed to lack skills in initiating movement, but he was given the opportunity to receive orientation and mobility instruction. Sam required four weeks of daily instruction to demonstrate competence in use of the public bus. When it was time for his "solo flight," I stood at the bus stop to bid him good-bye and good luck. The bus pulled up to the curb and the doors opened, but Sam would not go on the bus alone. He would not budge from his spot on the curb. The driver was patient enough to wait a few minutes while I talked to Sam, but Sam was adamant in his refusal to board that bus alone. A number of strategies were used to encourage, cajole, and coerce Sam to board the bus that day and subsequent days, but they all failed.

## The First Day of School

At the end of the first year of the orientation and mobility instruction, thirty-five pupils had learned to travel independently to the center. It was comforting to realize that an innovative program was successful. In early August, I was sprawled out on a blanket at the seashore, enjoying the summer sun and the smell and sound of the ocean crashing on the shore. As my mind wandered in a flight of sundry thoughts, I suddenly felt a sharp, prophetic pain of anxiety. How would the public transit riders manage on the first day of school, since they had not used the public bus all summer? Would there be thirty-five lost mentally retarded pupils wandering through the streets of Pittsburgh attempting to find the center? Would they forget everything they had learned? When I returned from my vaction, I called a number of the parents. They felt comfortable that their children would remember the route. I decided not to act but to wait for the first day of school to see what would happen. On that day, all thirty-five pupils arrived at the center.

### Clarence

Clarence had traveled successfully to the center for two weeks, and he was normally home by 4:20 PM. One day, his parents received a telephone call about 4:30 PM. It was Clarence. He said he fell asleep on the bus and passed his stop. He asked his father to pick him up with the family car. Clarence's father asked where he was, and Clarence responded by saying that he was in the phone booth. This was the only information that Clarence's father could get from him, that he was in the phone booth. His father got in the family car, followed the bus route, and eventually found Clarence; he was in a phone booth.

### The Tightrope Walker

In order to board her second bus, Laurie had to cross three streets in the downtown business district. In the early orientation and mobility lessons, Laurie did not know that pedestrians were required to cross streets at the corners. She seemed content to cross a street at just about any point. I explained that she must cross at corners, but she did not stay between the parallel pedestrian crosswalk lines. She would cross diagonally. "Laurie," I explained one day, "you must walk between the lines." She nodded her head as if to communicate understanding. When the light turned green, she stepped from the curb and placed her left foot carefully on one of the crosswalk lines, then she carefully placed her right foot directly in front of the left. She extended both arms out parallel to the ground to keep her balance and, with the care of a circus tightrope walker, walked on the one white line. I had to explain what I meant when I said, "walk between the lines."

## Wayne

Wayne approached me one morning and complained that for the past few days, some neighborhood kids were waiting for him when he got off the bus. They were teasing him. He related that the day before, one of the kids had punched him, and they had chased him home. He asked if he could take a different route home. I agreed and oriented him to a route that would involve use of a different bus. This seemed to solve the problem.

## John

Like other pupils who learned to travel independently to the center, it was the first time in his nineteen years that John had freedom to be on his own. But this freedom posed some problems for the center, for John's parents, and for John. We had problems getting John to arrive at the center on time in the morning. He enjoyed watching people walk by as he stood on the street corner. Another favorite activity of his, at least until he was caught, was to stand next to the morning newspaper vending machine and, when he had the opportunity, to steal newspapers. It was the type of vending machine where the purchaser would place his money in the slot, swing the door open, reach in for a paper, and then release the door, which sprung back to a locked position. After a person pulled out a newspaper, John would catch the door before it closed and pull out a free newspaper. He then would fold the newspaper, tuck it under his arm, and stand against a store-front. One day, the newspaper vendor caught him in the act of stealing the newspaper and chased him around the block.

## *Spiro*

Four years ago Spiro, at the time an obese seventeen-year-old, was prone to emotional, self-destructive outbursts. When frustrated, he would strike out at others and then subsequently at himself. For a period of time, he was excluded from the public schools and received homebound instruction. Soon his medication was changed, and he began a strict diet. He lost eighty pounds. Spiro's behavior improved considerably. He was readmitted to the center and eventually entered the center's vocational program. Subsequently, in a four-year period, he was able to contain his outbursts and attended the center without any disruptive incidents. Since Spiro's behavior had improved so radically — he was now twenty-one years old — and since this was his last year in the public school, it was decided to give Spiro an opportunity to learn transit travel skills. Because his family did not own a car, they relied solely on public transit for travel. Consequently, Spiro was quite accustomed to its use. His mother wanted Spiro to receive orientation and mobility instruction and was appreciative and cooperative with the efforts to teach him travel skills.

Spiro's early lessons demanded little from him. Initially, I accompanied Spiro through the travel route, and his first two lessons occurred without incident. Spiro followed directions and behaved quite appropriately. The third lesson went well until Spiro was about to alight from a bus near the center. Spiro was asked to give the bus driver his transfer before alighting from the bus. While standing by the driver he searched through the pockets of his pants, shirt, and coat. This took a few minutes, but I felt he had to learn to present his transfer upon alighting from the bus. After he could not find it, I gave him my transfer. Spiro gave it to the driver. When we alighted from the bus, I reminded him that he should always place his transfer in his wallet so he would know its location. I thought little of this incident, and we walked toward the center. Suddenly, Spiro began to wave his hands above his head and scream. We crossed a street and were directly in front of the center when Spiro began to violently hit his teeth with both hands formed in a fist. His gums began to bleed. I talked softly to him and encouraged him to relax so that we could go back to see his teacher. Spiro stopped his self-abusive behavior, and we returned to his classroom. As the result of this incident, I decided to terminate his orientation and mobility instruction so that Spiro's behavior could be observed further. I had to try to find some answers as to why this behavior occurred. Were there too many demands made on Spiro, or did some incident occur earlier in the day or week to set him off? Was he tense because he could not find his transfer? Answers were not available for these questions; however, his behavior stabilized during the next three weeks, and there were no further incidents. Because Spiro's behavior had progressed so well in the past four years, and because his mother had aggressively sought me to reinitiate instruction, I decided to give Spiro the benefit of doubt. We began travel instruction once again. What had occurred might have been an isolated incident, and I wanted to give Spiro another opportunity to prove he could travel independently. During the next week, Spiro and I met at the center in the morning and took the public bus to his home and then back to the center. Spiro behaved appropriately and learned the necessary skills to use the public bus. The next step was to have Spiro independently take the 7:30 AM bus from his neighborhood and alight downtown. I met him there and accompanied him the one block to the stop, where he waited for the second bus that took him to the center. After the school day he boarded the bus independently, and I met him downtown again so that I could observe this transfer of buses. This was successful, and at this point Spiro was semi-independent in that my only function was to observe his transfer of buses. Once on his second bus, Spiro traveled to his neighborhood alone, alighted, crossed a residential street, and walked home. Spiro was making excellent progress, and his behavior was appropriate.

Then, one afternoon while Spiro and I were downtown waiting for his second bus, a female acquaintance of Spiro's approached and began a nonstop monologue. She continued to talk to Spiro for what seemed like a lifetime, with an occasional question directed to Spiro. He just stood there, listening and answering her questions yes and no, but I could see that he was getting upset. Because I wanted to observe how Spiro would deal with this type of situation, I did not intervene and stood next to the pair as if I was just another person waiting for a bus. Suddenly Spiro started screaming and twice hit a plate glass window with the palms of his hands. He lunged at the female and held her in a bear hug. I pulled Spiro from the female and away from the plate glass window, but Spiro began to violently hit his teeth with his fists exactly like the earlier incident. I encouraged Spiro to begin walking, and soon he relaxed. As a result of this incident, Spiro was terminated from the orientation and mobility program, for the risk was too great that he might harm himself or others if another anxiety-provoking situation occurred during his travel. Apparently he had reached his tolerance level with the female, and the only way he knew to deal with his hostility was to let it out. Spiro certainly had the skills to travel independently on the public transit, but his unstable emotional outbursts disqualified him from independent travel.

### Harry

Harry left his home at 7:30 AM on his first "solo flight" to the center, but by 10:00 AM, he had not yet arrived. I decided to go to the downtown business district to trace Harry's travel route. My first stop was the bookstore, the point where Harry was to have alighted from his first bus. There he was, leaning against the bookstore display window. I walked up to Harry and congratulated him on reaching downtown. Very careful not to give Harry any verbal or nonverbal cues, I asked him what he had to do next in order to get to the center.

His eyes lit up and he said, "Oh Yeah."

Without saying another word, his body immediately started in a motion similar to what occurs when fresh batteries are placed in a child's toy. He walked to the corner of the block, crossed the street, and located the boarding point for his bus to the center. Since he had walked away from me, I observed from a distance as he boarded the correct bus. In a short time, he was at the center. My only intervention was to ask Harry what he had to do next. From the moment that Harry walked away from me, he was an independent traveler.

## Alan

Alan was a highly verbal pupil with a normal appearance. According to my evaluation, Alan was an excellent candidate of orientation and mobility instruction. On the first lesson, everything was fine until we alighted from the bus in his neighborhood. Soon after we began to walk the five blocks to locate his house, for no apparent reason, he began running. He ran off the sidewalk between two houses and was gone.

Once back at the center, I learned why Alan ran away from me. Alan was embarrassed to be walking in his neighborhood with me, since I was a teacher at his school. Alan was quite sensitive to the fact that he was enrolled at a "special" school. He thought that since he knew that I was a teacher in a "special" school, everyone would know, and he wanted to avoid embarassment. This problem was solved by my not accompanying him in his neighborhood.

Chapter 9

# THE PARENTS SPEAK _____

> ... The orientation and mobility program resulted in a whole
> new life for Peter. It is as major as toilet training or feeding
> for retarded people. Toilet training and self-feeding are those
> beginning steps in independence, and this is really the step
> into adulthood ...

Exerpt from· Parent Interview

THIS chapter is comprised of verbatim inter-
views with parents of pupils who have participated in orientation and mobility instruction. The interviews were conducted
in their homes, and each parent was interviewed separate from
his or her spouse. The parents talk candidly in retrospect about
the participation of their child in orientation and mobility
instruction and its effect on themselves, the family, and their
child. This chapter is included here to give professionals insight into the family dynamics involved when a child learns to
be an independent traveler, and it may be helpful to parents of
handicapped children who are considering involvement of their
child in an orientation and mobility program.

### PETER'S FATHER

*Q: What was your first reaction when you heard of the mo-
bility program?*
A: My son Peter had been going to school by taxi, and this had
been very convenient. When you first suggested that Peter
undertake a program that would involve him learning to
take the public transit to school, I was very skeptical. I just
never thought this kid could ride the public bus. That is
purely and simply it. Because I ride the bus to work every
day, I am familiar with the hazards. I go down to the
bottom of the hill and get the 81A, and it's a madhouse.

Sometimes it's so crowded you can't even get on the bus. You have to keep an eye open for when you want to get off. Because of all of these things, it was my initial impression that Peter could never do that. It seemed ridiculous even to think about it. His inadequacies would tend to be magnified by being in a situation where a lot of people are just intent on getting to work. I just couldn't feature Peter in an environment like that where his limitations would make it difficult for him. It's natural when you have a retarded child to try to keep him from being exposed to the rough side of life. I became less skeptical during the instructional process but was still very much an unbeliever until he was launched on his own and it went off without a hitch.

Q: *Why did you permit Peter to receive orientation and mobility instruction?*

A: Because I had faith in my wife's judgment of the school system's capability to not push him further than his capability. When you have a child with a handicap of any kind, you've got to have faith in those who know the whole community of handicapped people, and I figured that my wife and you folks know what you are doing. You are not making guinea pigs out of children. I thought it was ridiculous to teach Peter to ride the bus. You people who knew more about it made a different judgment. I was willing to go along with it. We have to commit ourselves to doctors, lawyers, and Indian chiefs, the experts in the society, and go along with their judgments. Sometimes things like this just don't work. I fully expected that someday my wife would say, "Well, we tried it with Peter, but he couldn't hack it." The best thing of all was the one time that I was up early enough to go in on the bus with Peter. For some reason — I really don't know what it was — we went down to the bus stop together. When the bus came, Peter fell into his regimen. He had his pass out to show the driver. He had a ticket, which he dropped into the box. We got on, and he seated himself up front, up close, and it was at a time when traffic wasn't as heavy as when I usually go in. There weren't that many people there. We sat there, and Pete kept looking. He wasn't diverted by his conversation with me. He was all business, and that's such an important thing for a limited child. To me, as a lay person, it seems important that they have those benchmarks for their whole existence. They are able to identify with places and times and things. I could see that he was having no trouble at all.

Q: *After Peter demonstrated success in traveling, what were some of your concerns?*

A: Well, I suppose the concerns you have for any youngster in a situation where he is vulnerable. Somebody may try to roll him or beat him up or taunt him just because some kids are human beings. They are mean, like the rest of us. But he never carried a great amount of money, and he is a good-natured fellow. I don't think I have any concerns. Even the time he got lost, I knew he was going to show up sooner or later. So I really wasn't concerned. I think it's a wonderful thing because it is giving him much more of a sense of a participation in everyday life. Who rides to school in a taxicab? You're different, there's something wrong, there's something different. Now he goes on the bus, and I suppose I still have residual concern that people look at Pete and say, "What's wrong with him — what's wrong with this kid on the bus here?" I do that. I see lots of people with irregularities or abnormalities. I look at them. They are different. But Pete doesn't mind it. Peter doesn't know he's all that different. He has a good sense of humor, so I really don't have that kind of concern. The thing I want to mention that impresses me from the point of view of being just a citizen and a taxpayer is the graphic illustration of what you do in terms of accomplishing a service and saving money. I don't know what the hell taxicab service costs, and I don't know what you make, but I know damn well that if you stack what the taxicab service costs against your fringe benefits and whatever, there's got to be a hell of a savings there. And in addition to that, you've got to be practical about that. People are not always going to buy a program that simply dignifies individuals, but they sure as the dickens are going to buy programs that have a demonstrable economic savings, and that's the dead solid perfect aspect of this program that really impresses me.

*Q: Has Pete's independent travel changed your perception of him?*

A: Sure. That's a thing he can do that I didn't think he could do, and it stretches our expectations of him, which isn't always good for him — it makes it tough for him. But that and learning to ride a two-wheel bike during the last year are two things that I never dreamed that child could do. It does change your perception. Here's a boy whose limitations are not as great as I thought they were because with a child like Peter I know there are severe limitations, and it's quite a triumph to overcome one by one the things that make him more able to be like a regular person.

*Q: Do you think he has changed his perception of himself? Does he act any differently as the result of independent travel?*

A: No, I can't say that. Peter has been very nonchalant about the whole thing. There are certain things in life you do, and you learn to ride the bus. It's not a big deal to him. It's kind of hard to tell because he doesn't have much ability to articulate his feelings. He was told he was going to ride the bus, and that's how he gets to school, and that's it. I am not at all an expert about retarded persons, but I do know of a capacity to focus on a single task that transcends what the normal person has because there are fewer distractions. If you give Pete a single thing to do, a single track to go on, he will really focus in on it. I don't know if that is true psychologically. It is just my observation, and I think that's one of the things that's happened here. Once he learned how to do it, he'll never forget. He knows the 81 A, B, C, and he knows his 16E bus. We speculated that the time he fouled up he may have been daydreaming or dawdling or got on the wrong bus, but I can see now that this wouldn't happen. It would have to be some external force that would divert him from that single-mindedness of purpose. So that is not a difference; it may be something that is highlighted by his experience. You give him something to do, and he either does it or it's something he can't do.

Q: *Do you have any further remarks?*

A: No, just to say to you what I said originally. The fact that Peter learned to use the public transit is really a miraculous thing for our family because our expectations were not high. It was a thrill that they have been stretched, to find that reality has stretched and reached beyond what our expectations are. Peter's done a thing that I never dreamed he would do. It changed my perception of him. For the moment, I am just extremely grateful that he has had this opportunity because today he could still be taking the cab, and that fact of his development and his normalization would be sadly neglected. I can think of lots of other kids who need this. That's the thing that hurts. Here's Peter who has a mom and dad who are fairly well educated and fairly perceptive about what's going on in our society, and particularly a mother who is just bound and determined that he's going to expand, to work up to his capacity. And I think of all those children who don't have those advantages and who don't have people like yourself and programs like the school systems here have, who are unnecessarily bound to a dependence that just fosters more dependence. The more dependent you make a child, the more dependent he is going to become. And by the same token, the more independent you make him, the more you can sit around and say, "What else can he do?" We never thought he could ride a bus; we never thought he could ride a two-wheel bike; what else can he do? That's what motivation can do. Look at all the opportunities that are lost, not only on retarded kids but on any kind of kid, because we're not seeing the real potential that everybody has. I really think this has been one of the most meaningful things for us, to have him acquire that degree of independence. It's a little bit to most people but to go down the hill, take the bus, and transfer is a lot to us.

## PETER'S MOTHER

*Q: What was your first reaction when you heard of the orientation and mobility program?*

A: Well, I heard about it at a parent meeting. Mrs. Johnson was so excited about it, and I was really interested in her and interested in what her son was doing and how pleased she was, but it didn't seem like something that related to me. It seemed like a wonderful thing that was happening to her child, and it was changing her life. I thought he was very able or much older. It was something I was very proud of for the retarded, but it wasn't something that was going to affect me.

*Q: What was your reaction when I first came and suggested that Peter receive orientation and mobility instruction?*

A: I guess I just really didn't believe that Pete was ready for it. Working in the field of retardation the way I do, almost all of the work I do is for other people. I don't think about it for Peter, and all of a sudden here was something that I had worked for; I mean I had been talking about you and telling people about you, Mike Laus, and all of a sudden now you were coming to me personally for my son and I couldn't believe it. All of us in the field work for other children, and all of a sudden our own child was involved, and I had a very different kind of feeling. I trusted you professionally because I had watched you for a year, and I know if you felt Pete was ready, he was ready. I never had any moment of doubt in you. I guess I just felt I was inadequate, our family was inadequate, and possibly Pete would be inadequate, but I never doubted you. And when you came and said that Pete was ready, I said OK.

*Q: Why did you say OK?*

A: Because I trusted you so much. I guess you might call me semi-professional in the field, and you gained my total confidence. It was only a matter of transferring my professional interest to my own child. Because of your style —

you have a very gentle sincere style — I knew that you cared as deeply for Peter as one could who was not a parent, and I knew you would not take chances with any child's life. I never thought of it 'til this moment, but it was because of you. I had watched you for about a year and listened to you for about a year, and then the last eight months of that year I had spoken about you to others and talked to others about you. In thinking about future parents of retarded children, I think an absolutely essential ingredient is that the parents feel that the mobility trainer cares. Someone could just approach a family and say, "I want to introduce you to Joe Smith, and he's going to train your kid." Whether that would work I don't know because that wasn't my experience, for I had known you way in the past.

Q: *What were some of your concerns during the orientation and mobility instruction?*

A: I guess we just all felt, we as a family felt, that we wanted to be useful, but we didn't quite know how to do it. You have made us so aware of Peter as an adult, as an emerging adult, and we have always thought of Peter as a child. You are the first professional who has made us aware of Peter in this new light. We are grateful for that, but that is a mixed bag. You know, it's much easier to think of your retarded child as a child and not as an adult. You have forced us into his adulthood, and that brings joys and sorrows. You always treat Peter as an adult, and we often don't. So that makes us feel inadequate. I guess I sort of resent you at moments because you treat him so much better than I do. Because you always treat him like an adult. We have a mixed feeling about you. You are so much more adequate with our kid than we can be, and yet I know I can be so much better with other people's kids than their parents can be. That's just a factor of parenthood, that you are so tied into a person emotionally that you can't always be the most effective person with him. I had trouble teaching my older son multiplication tables, but my sister-in-law could do it fine. So it's probably a pretty basic thing in parenting. So there were moments probably when I had a little resentment toward you. You have more patience as a style than I do. You are much more — passive isn't the right word — you're more patient than I am generally. I'm always rushing. I've always got more jobs on my mind than I should have, and I miss out in the depth relationship that you as a person have been able to establish. So I think I always feel a little inadequate when I'm working with you because I long to be more like you as a person. But you let the retarded person know that he is very very important, and I've hoped to do that with Pete, but my problem is that I have about sixteen other things I want to do too. By Peter's involvement in the program, all these feelings were brought out. I don't think I was ever fearful for Peter's safety. I really don't think that ever occurred to me. I think that's what people expect me to feel, and I didn't feel that. But what I felt was that this was an adult and none of us had ever treated him that way until now. We still have a long way to go in that way. The greatest problem for me, and I may be answering your next question, is Peter's lack of ability to communicate with me what goes on in the bus. I guess what I have said in the last three questions is that the training process made me feel inadequate as a parent. I've never thought about it until today.

Q: *How has this affected Peter? From your observation, is he acting any differently or does he have a different perception of himself?*

A: It's been very subtle. It's not been a Jekyll and Hyde kind of thing. For instance, he is trying to become more independent of me. This is just a minor example: he is very poor at washing his hair, but I keep trying to get him to do a better job and will add more soap or sneak in to look in the shower, and he will say "do it myself." We are going through an adolescent thing we should go through anyway at fifteen-and-a-half, but the independence he has learned probably added a little fuel to that fire, which is important for both people to go through. He's very confident on the street and I am sure his learning to ride the two-wheeler, which came at the same time, helped the whole experience.

He still keeps his street boundaries, but he'll be gone for long periods of time without checking in with the family. I noticed at a wedding yesterday that when a room is crowded, or he is in a very crowded situation, his landmarks are gone because there are so many people. He then becomes very dependent, and whereas he would usually go and ask for a Coke himself, he wanted me to go with him to ask for a Coke. One of the troubles about families is that they are not consistent. I mean I know he can go and get a Coke for himself, and then I'll suddenly go and ask for a Coke with him. Teachers, I think, are more consistent than families. Families at times treat these children like adults and at times treat them like children. It's probably hard to get mixed messages from the family, although everything is done in love. No matter what it is, it's done in a love context, and that might not be true in a school or in other situations, so I guess there's good from families too. Families have trouble measuring also because they see the person every day. People have noticed and commented to me on Peter's recent maturity. If someone hasn't seen him for a year, they are really shocked, but I can't isolate how much of that has come from the mobility experience because he is physiologically a man now where he was just emerging into that a year ago. I think the biggest change is in the way we treat Peter more than in how Pete has changed. He's done something that people didn't think he could do, and that's kind of a neat feeling for him. We're all proud. When someone is getting D's in English and he pulls an A, the whole family is proud when he pulls it out. Well, Pete pulled one out on us. He really did a job. All of us around Pete have tremendous pride. It's kind of like an athlete — gosh, he did it!

Q: *Do you have any further remarks?*
A: I just want to tell you how grateful we are to you and the program. The orientation and mobility program resulted in a whole new lease on life for Peter. It is as major as toilet training or feeding for retarded people. Toilet training and self feeding are those beginning steps in independence, and

this is really the step into adulthood. It's important to let families know how absolutely essential the step is into the adult world. There is really no way I can say it any stronger than that. The interesting irony of it — and I don't know whether you've talked about this in your book or not — is that its not only the most compassionate and educationally sound thing for the adult retarded person, but is saves tax-payers money because our family estimated that the cab that used to pick up Pete cost six to eight dollars a day for Pete to go to school and now he goes for forty-five cents each way or ninety cents per day. If people really didn't care about people, at least it saves money. And there are so many other ways it affects retarded persons. He has a sense of who he is in the world. Pete lets me know when he is not safe or not happy, and I don't think Peter would have participated in the program if he didn't think he could do it. There were times when he refused to do things. Maybe it's because he didn't have a good teacher like you, but I think the retarded person would let the trainer know he couldn't do the task, and there are ways to communicate that to you. I guess you're kind of like I am. I am absolutely amazed how able our retarded people are; there is such a great resource there that we have not tapped. It's our inadequacies, not the retarded person's inadequacies, that are holding us back. Our inadequacy lies in how to approach the person, how to help him, and how to help him help himself.

## BETSY'S MOTHER

Q: *What was your first reaction when I suggested that Betsy be trained to ride the public bus?*

A: Wow, scared to death, scared to death! I never thought she would learn it in such a hurry. I mean, when you said you were going to teach, I figured that it would be months. When you came two weeks later and said she was going by herself, I almost dropped dead. No, never in this world did I think she would be able to do it. When she got lost, that was really the worst. But then, once she learned — well, now I don't have any fears. Well, I wouldn't say I didn't have any fears about her going but I let her go knowing, hoping, that she comes back alright, and I know she won't get lost going where she is. If she went somewhere else, she would get lost, you know, until she was trained, but the way she goes now, why, she has it down pat.

Q: *How long has she been riding the bus by herself?*

A: I think, yes, about two years since you taught her to go by herself. I would say it really didn't take her that long to get used to it. And I know she got lost that first day and that a couple of times she fell asleep and rode past her stop, but she had sense enough to get off and call up and say, "I'm here, Dad. Come and get me." You know, she waited until her dad went and got her. But like I said, I was really surprised that she did it as well as she did. I still never figured out how she knew where to get off at Woodland Street, but she had to have some kind of sign. What it was, I don't know. I thought maybe it was that yellow house, but I don't know. She never would tell me. If she rides home on the bus with somebody now, like her sister, or if someone happens to meet her, she won't let them say when to get off. She gets off the bus by herself.

Q: *As the result of her success, have you looked a little differently at Betsy?*

A: Well, I think so because I think that until she had this training — of course, when she went to the private school she had a lot of training, but she never learned to go anywhere by herself or anything like that — I never expected that she would ever be able to someday take care of herself, and that she might be able to do better than she would have if she never had that training. Because then where would she have been? She would have had to stay in the house all by herself. This way, she can take the chance and venture out somewhere. So I think it changed our attitude a lot, as far as what she might be able to and not be able to do.

To tell you the truth, when she was born, I never had any idea what it would be like, I didn't even know that's what she was when she was born. Even my doctor didn't tell me in the hospital. She got real sick after we brought her home; she almost died. Our pediatrician came out that morning and said, "You know, she's different than your other children." We said, "Why? What do you mean?" And she told me. I didn't even know. I didn't even know. Then she got on the phone and called my doctor and said, "Why did you let this woman go home without telling her that her daughter was, you, know, the way she is?" He just had no interest. He never said a word. And I didn't know it until she told me. But like I said, I have a lot more confidence in her now, since you've had her in this program.

*Q: How about Betsy? Do you think she has changed her feelings about herself? Do you think she has developed some confidence?*

A: Oh, I think so! Oh, yeah! I guess if we would have the nerve to let her do more things than what she does now, she would do them. She has more confidence in herself, too, since she rides the bus and that. And like I say, she wants to go to church by herself. The first time she said that, I thought, "Oh, no!" Then I thought to myself, "Well, gee, she rides the bus every day, and all she has to do is walk down the hill and she's at church." So she likes to go to church by herself. I guess that she has a lot more confidence in herself, a lot more than she would have had, because like I said, we would have been scared to let her do anything. It makes a difference.

*Q: Has it made a difference as far as her job, being able to get a job?*

A: Oh, yeah, and being able to make some money the same as everybody else, and having a payday — she looks forward to that, her paydays. She'll say to her dad, "Guess what Friday is, Dad?" Then she'll say "Guess what Tuesday is?" I know that made a big difference. She has her own money to spend. Oh, yeah, because she probably never would have had it other than that. So it makes a lot of difference — that independence and just knowing that she can do something and that it's not all for nothing. I think it's a lot.

*Q: Are there any other further remarks, or anything you would like to say?*

A: Well, of course, right now I guess I can't think of anything. Her sisters and brother help her a lot, try to teach her things. She wants to be all up on the modern stuff. She never would go out by herself, and even when she first started going to the sheltered workshop — they had those dances and that — she would never want to go until I think it was this last Christmas. This young girl, all I know her by is "Joan," said she was Betsy's friend, and she lives around here on Davis Avenue, and she talked her into going to the dance. Since then, she goes whenever they have the things, and she loves it. They just had a dance there, a formal dance, not long ago, and she loved it. She loves to dance. She's pretty good at it! I think that what you've done for her has made her altogether different than she would have been. Really, I do. She wouldn't have been nearly ... I know if it had depended on us, because like I said, we would have been afraid to do anything like that, she wouldn't have come so far.

*Q: What message would you give to other parents? What would you say to them if you had a chance, about orientation and mobility instruction for their children?*

A: Oh, well, I would say definitely don't be afraid to let them go. Don't be afraid. Because I can see what it has done for her. Like I say, when she got lost, and I had to let her go the next day and the girls told me, "Oh, Mother, you're not going to let her go again, are you?" I was scared to death, but I said, "I have to. If I don't, that's the end of it — she'll never learn." Oh, yes, I would definitely tell them to let them go. Definitely. Because it's a big thing, a really big thing. At least, I think it is. It's hard, but once you get used to it, it's alright. I would say yes, definitely yes, because it makes a big difference, not only to yourself, but to the child, too. It makes a big difference. It gives her a sense of confidence, I think, and a sense of being somebody, not just nothing, that she can't do this, she can't do that, and I think it gives her an incentive to try a little bit harder to learn things. I say let them try whatever they want to try, even though you're scared, let them try. It's a big thing, I think.

### BETSY'S FATHER

*Q: How did you first hear about the mobility program?*

A: Well, it was through the center, and I imagine it was through you that we heard about this program of traveling. It came up that you were going to train her to ride the bus. It was hard to take at first, or even think about, because actually — well, one time before, when she was tested for that place on Forbes Street, they said she would have to ride the bus — we thought it was utterly impossible for a child like that to ride the bus, so we just didn't; we couldn't possibly at that time, feel that it was anything ... we just didn't enroll her in the program.

But then, naturally, when you came out to talk to us about it, we laid some of the fears ... and the first few days were rather hectic, and then when she did get lost a couple of times it was something, but she did alright. She knew to call up. The only thing, it was odd that one time she forgot to tell me where she was. She said "I'm in a gas station on Brighton Road." So I didn't know whether she was way out or way in, but I found her. She was at the Esso station past Milton Street, just waiting and expecting me. Just like she was the time she took her bike and rode down McKnight Road as far as the sidewalk goes. She parked her bike then, and she was waiting for me! But it all turned out alright. But this ability to travel herself has done a world of good for her. She really enjoys going out.

I have offered to drive her different times, but she would rather go her routine. Once in a while, she'll ask me for a ride over to the bus. She'll say, "I need a ride, Dad." So then I ride her over to Brighton Road and she goes on the bus.

Then, by the same token, there is a friend of ours who

sees her there, and she would pick her up and take her over, but that's no good. It's better to let her have her routine and go on her bus, and then she's alright.

Q: *When I first suggested that, how did you feel?*

A: Well, our first reaction was negative. Of course, we didn't realize, really think that it could be. You envision all kinds of things, and then one of the factors with Betsy was her lack of communication. You know she has a little trouble getting the words out. And that makes you wonder too, but she seems to get along quite well. She has no problems. She can go early or late or whatever, and it doesn't shake her up anymore. Whatever there is, why, that's what she does.

Q: *Do you look at Betsy any differently since she has learned to travel independently?*

A: Oh, it took her out of the more or less "helpless group," and she's now just like any other working nut. She'll go home, go to work, come home ... and she gets a big, well, every day she gets a big greeting. You know, of course, that payday — that's ... she's all pleased. Big deal. But without that, I mean, she would be left out. She would get disgusted because as you can see, she's active. I mean, after all, you struggle long enough, and that seems to be the key with people like Betsy. It's there for them, but it takes more doing and more patience, more understanding to get it across. It's very slow. I show her keys on the guitar and she'll get ... It used to be I didn't pay any attention. I just let her do anything. But I don't let her do that anymore. I show her the C chord. Of course, I don't play it myself. I just got it out of the book. I showed her the C, G, D7 and then make her do her homework with E, F, G, and all that jazz. But I figure that in time she'll know where they're at and understand it. And once she gets the picture in her mind, why, she'll be able to chord it a little bit, which would be fun for her. It just takes time. That's the thing. It takes so long.

Q: *If you had a chance to talk to other parents of retarded children, who may have the chance for mobility training, what would you tell them?*

A: I would tell them to think about it very seriously, to give their child the advantage of the training, because there is no way you can really express what it does for them. It just widens their world, makes them feel that they're like everybody else. Actually, everybody likes to travel, no matter who it is, and they much more so. Everything that they do is an experience, especially if they can accomplish something that everybody else does, and then they feel more like they belong. That's one of the dangerous things about people like Betsy. If they get to thinking that they are in a lesser group, it is very damaging to their ego and their whole mental make-up. So I really am certainly glad that we saw fit to let her learn. It gives her a reasonable life. I mean, she can be active. If it wouldn't have happened, she would be just home all the time. You get tired of doing nothing — you have four walls upstairs and downstairs — you get disgusted. She's getting older; she's twenty-two years old. This way she has the incentive to save her money to go to the concert to see Elvis. It gives her something to shoot at.

When somebody is going out in that direction either myself, my wife, or one of the relatives, we'll take her along, and she'll see if Elvis is out there. Of course, I never know how she's going to feel after her bank account goes down, whether she can accept that! But I imagine well, she realizes that she spends money. She knows.

Every once in a while I give her a glass of wine. She's twenty-two years old, you know. She'll ask for a glass of wine once in a while. I give it to her. She'll buy a bottle of wine. She'll say, "I'll buy a bottle, Dad." I didn't want her to, but then I figured, why not? After all, she has to learn that too, that she spends some money, so I let her buy a bottle of wine. But she really doesn't know. I mean, she'll drink a glass of wine, just one glass, and about fifteen minutes later, she'll take a glass of pop. I think she likes the pop, but she drinks the wine because she's twenty-two years old, and she likes to feel that she's able to do that.

Without her travel, I really hate to think what it would be

like. You kind of tend to not really think about it too much. But just the other day I was thinking about it, and I was so glad that she does it. I have a friend that I work with; his boy was in very bad shape, and he's in an institution. When he has time off, he and his wife go up there to see the kid. He's in bad shape. John goes up there to see him and he says, "Your daughter is something." It's really kind of sad, you know, but I always ask him about his boy, and he always asks me about Betsy also.

They have done wonders with that boy. He couldn't take care of himself or anything, but he's going up to that school. He takes care of his clothes, he's trained, goes to the bathroom, takes his bath and everything. Of course, he and his wife go up to see him. It's there, but it takes the patience and the time, such as you've put into this. It's just like one step at a time. It isn't done all together; you take it apart and put it together.

### STEVE'S FATHER

*Q: What was your first reaction when it was first suggested that Steve begin orientation and mobility training?*

A: Well, I was totally sure that he could do this, but my wife was very leery of it.

*Q: Why did you feel confident?*

A: I believe that Steve's capabilities are much greater than what people give him credit for.

*Q: Did you have any concerns during the instructional process?*

A: After the original incident of him getting lost, I was very much concerned for maybe three or four days.

*Q: Would you explain what you mean by that one incident?*

A: He didn't come home until about 9:00 that evening, and everybody was out hunting for him — relatives, police, just about everybody I knew. It was very upsetting. I myself was riding around just aimlessly, because I didn't want to come here, knowing he wasn't here. I guess that would be about it.

*Q: Why did you let him try it again the next day?*

A: My wife was very much against this. I knew that he had to have something to do the rest of his life. He just couldn't sit around the house. I was very much in favor of what was being done to get him something to do during the day, and I think from this experience that he could possibly progress to doing something else. So I was bound and determined to do whatever I had to do. If I had to do it myself to make sure he was safe, I would have done this.

*Q: Has what Steve accomplished changed him in any way?*

A: No, I don't honestly think that it has changed him to any great degree. I think he is much happier being able to go to work. He just does like anybody else does. He sometimes says he doesn't want to do to work, but I think he's very happy in what he is doing. Just basically, I think Steve's a pretty happy child.

*Q: This is a little out of order, but jumping back to that incident when he got lost, what was your reaction? How did you feel about me during that time and the program?*

A: Well, now, just being honest with you, you were lucky you ain't around me, because I got a very quick fuse.

*Q: What was going through your mind?*

A: I kind of deal harshly with things, you might say, maybe because of my job or type of business I'm in. But I was really upset.

*Q: Did you feel that I didn't do my job?*

A: Yeah, I thought you let him go too quick. That if this happened, and without a doubt it did happen, I think you made a very critical error in judgment. I thought that he was given the go-ahead too quick to do what he was put up to do.

I do think from the outset that I had faith that he could do this. I was very surprised myself that he did get lost. Of course, all kind of things run through your mind, especially in the Pittsburgh neighborhood right around that area, particularly the many buses. When I went down to that corner and looked at them buses and where they were going, I thought, "Oh boy, oh boy." I know the different areas to which the buses travel and the buses he could have got on. Then I was very disturbed. With the way people are today, God only knows what they would do with a little fellow like that, have fun with him, torture him, God only knows.

Q: *Do you still think we pulled too soon?*

A: I really can't say what happened. I really don't have no idea why he didn't get on that bus, whether it was a crowded bus, whether something alarmed him on that particular bus, because he has apparently done it without a hitch every time since then.

Q: *If you had a chance to speak to other parents, what would you tell them about the mobility program?*

A: I would definitely encourage them to take a shot at it. I guess each parent would judge their own kid's capabilities a little bit different, but I believe as long as they feel security in their own mind that the kid is capable of doing it, without a doubt they should go along with it for the very reason that I did — just for the fact of giving them something to do, getting them out of the house, and letting them help contribute in their own way to what's going on in the world. In fact, many times I had thought of getting a car wash or something; Steve likes to wash automobiles; and just running it with retarded children, because I do believe they have capabilities that are over and above what they're really showing in these different places.

Q: *Is there anything further you would like to say?*

A: Nothing really to do with mobility, transportation wise. But I really honestly and sincerely feel that there really is not enough being done for children of Steve's nature. I believe that their capabilities are a little bit higher, and I think that they could gain employment of maybe a little greater nature than what they have now. Like Steve specifically likes to cut grass and do things of this nature. I haven't cut the grass around here for quite some time, and he does the house next door and a couple up the street. He makes a few dollars at it. The fact is, it keeps him busy, and when he's busy he's happy, because he don't have relationships with other young children. He'll play with this neighborhood kid, and they all have their own interests which would be outside of Steve's, and he really has no friends, other than me. He's very close to me. So just basically, I think a lot more could be done than what is being done. The answer to this — I don't know the answer to it. I think it is going to progress as years go by. I see a lot more than when Steve started. A lot more is being done with children of this nature than was being done years ago.

I can't judge other children, but he's a steady worker, and he goes every day. I imagine jobs suited to his nature would be maybe making boxes or whatever children like this could do. I imagine that a fellow with a higher degree of intelligence would not find this work very interesting, and I imagine there is a lot of absenteeism and things like that. Steve goes to work every day and seems to enjoy it. Like all people with jobs, he raises hell, "I don't want to go, the hell with that; it's too hot," and this and that, just like anybody else with any job does.

Maybe we're fortunate inasmuch as Steve is pretty well accepted. For some reason or other, the bus drivers seem to like him, and the people in the neighborhood are all friendly to him. We really haven't had a problem where we as parents had to put up with any kind of bullcrap. So he seems to be smiling all the time. From what other people tell me — one of our friends goes on the bus, or did go on the bus with him before they changed the time Steve had to be there — and she says the bus driver keeps him a seat there and always kids with him just like everybody always seems to do after they get to know Steve a little bit. So I think he's done really well by it, and I know my wife didn't want to go through this; in other words, she was dead set against it that night. We had a hell of an argument. I said, "He's going to go on the bus in the morning," and she really raised hell. She was hysterical. I was worried and very much concerned that she was going to blow her lid. So we had a pretty good spat over it that night, and I guess in front of all the relatives, too, because she was insisting he wasn't going to go, and I definitely was insisting he was. You had to give it a chance. You got to do it for his future because I could well realize what would happen if he had to be around this house all day. So I am appreciative, and I am very glad that it worked out the way it did. In all probability, you did do your job, and I maybe jumped to conclusions with what I thought.

### STEVE'S MOTHER

*Q: What was your first reaction when I approached you about teaching Steve to travel independently?*

A: Well, first of all, I really had no other choice because my husband insisted on it. I think I would have been afraid to go through with it, as much as I would have wanted to, if it had been my own decision.

*Q: What were your biggest concerns about Steve riding the bus by himself?*

A: Well, first of all, he has never been on his own, other than on our street. We have taken him everywhere in a car and with us, but he has never been on his own off this street. I've never even let him go down to the shopping center or anything. He's been up and down the street, and that's it.

One time, when he was younger and I didn't drive, I had to bring him home from school on the bus. When he went to get on the bus, he started screaming, and he wouldn't get on it. But I think it was the noise of the bus, and he wouldn't get on, so I had to take a cab home, and ever since then I just would never take him on the bus. So that's one of the reasons I never thought he would want to take the bus.

*Q: How old was he then?*

A: Oh, I'd say he was about maybe nine or ten. It's been a good while back. So I never really thought he would even ride it. Steve sort of has no confidence in himself, and he has to be forced to do things, but I think this has given him confidence. I really can see the difference in him. I noticed right after he did start to ride that he had more of an air of independence. Not only me, but my relatives did too because my sister used to say, "Gee, doesn't Steve seem like he's more sure of himself and proud of himself, really?" I think it made a big impact on him. I think it's done a lot for him.

Q: *What were some of your concerns?*

A: My concern was mostly ... although I thought that Steve has a good memory and he could remember how to go, but I was a little worried about him maybe meeting the wrong people and somebody swaying him the wrong way, and I still have this concern a little bit. I try to teach him not to go with strangers and that, but it still is with me, although it is diminishing since I see that he's been doing it over a year now.

Q: *Are there any other concerns besides that?*

A: No, not really, because I think now he has got it down pat.

Q: *But back when he started to travel independently, what were you thinking?*

A: I was worried about him maybe getting on the wrong bus, maybe his mind not paying attention. Where he gets his bus, there's about four or five buses sometimes right behind each other. So I was concerned about that, maybe getting the wrong bus and getting off in the wrong neighborhood.

My concern mostly with Steve is being that he don't talk. If he could speak — this was the main reason why I didn't want to send him. What if he gets lost, how is he going to tell somebody? And that's really — I didn't think you would be able to teach him. I think I did tell you that he doesn't speak, and I asked you how you would teach him. If he got lost, how could he tell somebody, "I'm lost"? So that's a concern still, because if something does happen — you know, it hasn't happened yet.

Q: *You did answer a question I had in mind — have you seen a difference in Steve?*

A: I really have. This has done more for Steve than anything. I can see him now — he's even trying to speak more; he says more. In fact, every once in a while — the ones that will notice it are the relatives, because he is around us all and that. But like my sister will come in and he'll start to say, like, sentences, and I think he is getting more confidence in himself. I do, I think this has been one of the best things that could happen to Steve, really, because now I think he can do more than he actually does.

### MARK'S FATHER

Q: *What was your first reaction when I suggested that Mark begin orientation and mobility instruction?*

A: I was afraid to let him on his own. I was afraid to make him go back and forth to town or wherever he had to go. It was something that I didn't think I would have the guts to let him do. I didn't think that he would be able to do it. In fact, even before this I would not permit him to do much alone, and I did most things for him. I never dreamed that Mark could travel to the center or go to town or travel on any public vehicle by himself. I didn't think he could do it, and I was afraid to allow him to do it. And I really felt that perhaps I should take him back and forth to school all the time to get him away from being with other people.

Q: *What were some of your concerns about Mark eventually traveling independently to the center?*

A: I think the first thing that hit me was that if he had to travel by himself, he would not be alert enough to cross the street safely. He might not look both ways and would not know when a car had his turn signals on to turn right. My first fear was that he just wouldn't be safe. My second fear was perhaps he would get on the wrong bus, and he would get lost. I just couldn't see him recognizing the bus numerals, getting on the bus, using correct change, getting off, walking several blocks, getting on another bus, getting to his appointed destination; and the same on the return trip.

Q: *What made you decide when you did? What went through your mind in coming up with that decision?*

A: Well, one day he would have to do this by himself, when either I or his mother or his brothers would not be there to shelter him the way that I have tried to do, and I finally realized that. And after meeting you, I had the confidence that I should have had in the beginning, and that kind of made me go along. There was a doubt whether I should allow it or not because of my own fears. I guess I figured I had to give him a chance to show me what he could do.

Q: *As a result of Mark's success, have you looked at him in a different way or had a different perspective?*

A: Oh yes. There are many things that I feel he can do now that I never gave him a chance to do, and there are many things that I stopped doing for him that I let him do himself now. I would not let him go to a store, even to cross one street, and I now send him down to the store, and I don't worry about him not returning safe or not being able to cross the street or anything like that.

Q: *Do you feel that his success in independent travel made the difference?*

A: Oh yes, I never dreamed that Mark would go to school or to town or travel on any vehicle by himself. I didn't think that he would do it because I was afraid to let him do it until I was shown by you that he could do it.

Q: *Have you seen any differences or any changes in Mark as a result of his accomplishment?*

A: Being more grown-up and feeling more secure. I know there were times when I would go down to the bus — I even do it now — and he looks at me like "What are you doing here?" — as if he couldn't do it himself. Now he is grown, he is more adult, more his age now, he acts more his age. And this is because he's gotten this thing that he can travel by himself.

Q: *What advice would give to other parents of retarded children in regards to orientation and mobility instruction?*

A: I would tell them to try not to be as fearful as they are, because things do work out. I mean, with as much time as they need, they will learn, and that it is most important.

Q: *How do you feel about Mark's future, realizing that he now is an independent traveler?*

A: I used to worry about what would happen to him when I am not here, but I don't worry as much; put it that way. I don't; I used to worry about him from morning to night, all the hours that I was awake about, you know, this thing traveling, but now I am more relaxed. I don't worry about what is going to happen to Mark too much anymore. I am not saying that because you are sitting there; I am talking seriously; I mean that sincerely. And it all stems from him traveling by himself, which is one of the greatest things that has happened to him.

Q: *What qualities do you think are important, that made you comfortable about a person like me coming in?*

A: Well, number one, your manner, which I think is very good, and you can usually tell when someone has the patience. It is hard to have feeling and patience for a child, man, like Mark, a stranger, or for someone who has not lived with one like that or has raised one. And you don't think that there is anyone who can feel the way you feel, well, whom you can put your trust in. That is what we did. Even after my wife and I decided to go ahead and try this out I felt very comfortable. Mark in your hands was alright with me. To really put into words, you know how you feel about what Mark has done; it's a joyous thing. You can't say joy; you feel it inside of you, and to bring it out into words ... What's that saying about you can't put it into words? Well I just can't put it into words. And you can see what expressions you have found in my wife and I.

## MARK'S MOTHER

Q: *What was your first reaction when it was suggested that Mark receive orientation and mobility instruction?*

A: I was a little frightened, and the principal told me that most parents were, you know, so I was a little convinced but not all the way. But then after you came, we could see the warmth about you, and you really made us feel confident after we started talking. I thought he had to learn sometime. And when you insisted that he would be alright, we thought we would take the chance, and we are really grateful for that.

*Q: What were some of your concerns once Mark was traveling independently?*

A: Frankly, I was worried about somebody taking advantage of him. I didn't know whether he was capable. To be honest, we weren't the type to really let him go out on his own much. And when you called me and told me that you were sending him home by himself, well, I don't know how I went through the day, really. And when he came home with a smile on his face, I had a bigger one on mine because I never thought it could happen, really. I've seen the biggest difference in him since he knows that he can come and go by himself. And I don't even think about it anymore, I really don't. I mean, a couple of times he came home later than he should have, and I always give him money to call us. And this one day he didn't call, and I was a little worried, but then I thought, well, I am sure he knows what he is doing. And here's what happened. He had met his dad in town, and that is why he is late. But he knows enough not to talk to strangers and stuff like that.

*Q: You mentioned that it made a difference in Mark, would you talk a bit more about that?*

A: I think that he is proud of himself now that he has learned to be responsible for his travel. And like I said before, we never gave him this chance; we always were with this fear, you know, that maybe he couldn't do it, never trying him out to see if he could do it. And if it weren't for you, we still wouldn't have let him go like that. And now he knows he can, and he wants to do more than what he did before. He'll take a try at anything now where he didn't before because we never expected it of him. And I find this with anything that he wants to do. I mean, we will suggest something, and he'll always say no; but if we keep at him, and once he tries something and sees that he can do it, then he is more at ease with it.

Q: *Do you think his success in travel has changed your perception of him?*

A: Definitely. I never thought he was capable. I never thought he really was. Just knowing he can do that, I feel that there is more things that he can do. And I thought if he can travel himself, there's a lot of other things he can do. I never expected anything from him in the way of doing things around the house, and now I tell him to run the sweeper, which I never would have thought to ask him before, and he is capable of helping out in the lawn with his dad. He is capable. I feel that he is an all-around more grown-up person since I know he can do this. He has told me that he even has gone into stores, you know, like he will browse around. But he knows that he has to call before he goes to do something like this.

Q: *Does he do that often?*

A: Not too often. Like if he knows it is somebody's birthday or something, then he will tell us that he went and looked around to see if there was something that he could get for the person. Fortunately, his dad works in town and they have met, you know, and they go shopping or have something cool to drink, and then he tells him to come home on a bus. And he comes straight home.

Q: *In looking to the future, do you think his success in mobility has made you feel a bit more at ease?*

A: Definitely, yes. I feel that it has really done a lot for him. I really do. I think he is more sure of himself, really.

Q: *What would you say to other parents regarding orientation and mobility instruction?*

A: Oh, I definitely would tell them to go right ahead. And I would also tell them that they might have this fear behind their minds at first. But someone as warm-hearted as you — when you come into our home and made us feel like he belonged to you as well as to us — was enough for me. And I would advise any parent to go ahead and let their child learn this. I feel that it is the biggest step for them, I really do.

Q: *What qualities of a person coming into your house make you trust them?*

A: When you came to our house, I could see the warmth about you. You made us feel confident. After our discussion, I thought that Mark had to learn sometime. When you insisted that he would be safe, we felt we would take the chance. I am grateful for that. When you visited us, it was your attitude that impressed us. A lot of people in the field of mental retardation are cold. I don't think they mean to be this way, but they feel that they know what they are talking about, and they just go on and say, "You should do this and you should do that." You didn't act that way. You came in and made us feel like Mark belonged to you as well as us. You gave us a choice. You made us feel that what you were telling us was true, or you wouldn't have been sitting here and telling it to us. This is what made me feel that you were capable of teaching my son to travel. You were warm and understanding about everything. You explained to us that you understood the situation, and you said that most people do have this fear. You said that once you let Mark go, he would be capable of more things than we thought. And I found this to be true. You didn't come in and say, "Well, I'm going to teach Mark mobility." You didn't do this. You gave us a choice. That's what made us feel more secure. I think it was the way you went about it really. You talked to us like you knew us. This I think is important. Especially with our child being like this, we are constantly worrying, and when someone makes us feel secure enough, there's such a difference, you know, from when somebody acts cold, and they come in and say, "Well, we are teaching mobility, and you should just let your son go out." I mean, you didn't insist on it. And that is what made me feel more secure about you.

# REFERENCES _____

Argyris, C.: *Intervention Theory and Method: A Behavioral Science View.* Reading, A-W, 1970.

Ball, M. J.: Mobility in perspective. *Blindness 1964 AAWB Annual,* pp. 107-141, 1964.

Conant, R. C.: Personal communication, May 21, 1976.

Cortazzo, A. C. and Sansone, R.: Travel training. *Teaching Exceptional Children, 3:*67-82, 1969.

De Cecco, J. P.: *The Psychology of Learning and Instruction: Educational Psychology.* Englewood Cliffs, P-H, 1968.

Gilbert, T. F.: Mathetics: the technology of education. *The Journal of Mathetics, 1:*7-73, 1962.

Groce, M. M.: *Travel Training for the Handicapped.* Evaluation report. New York, Board of Education of the City of New York, 1973.

Hogan, R. C.: *The Rationale, Design, Implementation, and Evaluation of a Composition Program Employing Backward Sequence.* Unpublished doctoral dissertation, University of Pittsburgh, 1975.

Kubat, A.: Unique experiment in independent travel. *J Rehabil, 2:*36-39, 1973.

Laus, M. D.: Orientation and mobility instruction for the sighted trainable mentally retarded. *Education and Training of the Mentally Retarded, 9:*70-72, 1974.

Perske, R.: The dignity of risk. In Wolfensberger, W. (Ed.): *The Principle of Normalization in Human Services.* Toronto, National Institute on Mental Retardation, 1972.

President's Committee on Mental Retardation: *Transportation and the Mentally Retarded.* Washington, D.C., National Center for Educational Research and Development (DHEW/OE), 1972. (ERIC Document Reproductional Service No. ED 064 841).

Tobias, J.: *Training for Independent Living.* New York, Association for Help of Retarded Children, 1963.

Welsh, R. L.: Cognitive and psychosocial aspects of mobility training. *Blindness 1972 AAWB Annual,* pp. 99-109, 1972.